William Faulkner's
THE SOUND AND THE FURY

CURRENTLY AVAILABLE

The Adventures of Huckleberry Finn
Mark Twain

Aeneid
Vergil

Animal Farm
George Orwell

The Autobiography of Malcolm X
Alex Haley & Malcolm X

Beowulf

Billy Budd, Benito Cereno, & Bartleby the Scrivener
Herman Melville

Brave New World
Aldous Huxley

The Catcher in the Rye
J. D. Salinger

Crime and Punishment
Fyodor Dostoevsky

The Crucible
Arthur Miller

Death of a Salesman
Arthur Miller

The Divine Comedy (Inferno)
Dante

A Farewell to Arms
Ernest Hemingway

Frankenstein
Mary Shelley

The Grapes of Wrath
John Steinbeck

Great Expectations
Charles Dickens

The Great Gatsby
F. Scott Fitzgerald

Gulliver's Travels
Jonathan Swift

Hamlet
William Shakespeare

Heart of Darkness & The Secret Sharer
Joseph Conrad

Henry IV, Part One
William Shakespeare

I Know Why the Caged Bird Sings
Maya Angelou

Iliad
Homer

Invisible Man
Ralph Ellison

Jane Eyre
Charlotte Brontë

Julius Caesar
William Shakespeare

King Lear
William Shakespeare

Lord of the Flies
William Golding

Macbeth
William Shakespeare

A Midsummer Night's Dream
William Shakespeare

Moby-Dick
Herman Melville

Native Son
Richard Wright

Nineteen Eighty-Four
George Orwell

Odyssey
Homer

Oedipus Plays
Sophocles

Of Mice and Men
John Steinbeck

The Old Man and the Sea
Ernest Hemingway

Othello
William Shakespeare

Paradise Lost
John Milton

Pride and Prejudice
Jane Austen

The Red Badge of Courage
Stephen Crane

Romeo and Juliet
William Shakespeare

The Scarlet Letter
Nathaniel Hawthorne

Silas Marner
George Eliot

The Sun Also Rises
Ernest Hemingway

A Tale of Two Cities
Charles Dickens

Tess of the D'Urbervilles
Thomas Hardy

To Kill a Mockingbird
Harper Lee

Uncle Tom's Cabin
Harriet Beecher Stowe

Wuthering Heights
Emily Brontë

William Faulkner's
THE SOUND AND THE FURY

Bloom's NOTES

A CONTEMPORARY
LITERARY VIEWS BOOK

Edited and with an Introduction by
HAROLD BLOOM

Introduction © 1999 by Harold Bloom

Printed and bound in the United States of America.

3 5 7 9 8 6 4 2

The hardback of this edition has been cataloged as follows:

Library of Congress Cataloging-in-Publication Data

The sound and the fury / edited & with an introduction by Harold Bloom.
p.   cm. — (Bloom's notes)
Includes bibliographical references (p.   ) and index.
ISBN 0-7910-4519-6 (hc). — ISBN 0-7910-4569-2 (pb)
1. Faulkner, William. 1897-1962. Sound and the fury–
–Examinations—Study guides. I. Bloom, Harold. II. Series.
PS3511.A86s858 1998.
813'.52—dc21
98-2807
CIP

Chelsea House Publishers
1974 Sproul Road, Suite 400
Broomall, PA 19008-0914

Contents

User's Guide

This volume is designed to present biographical, critical, and bibliographical information on the author and the work. Following Harold Bloom's editor's note and introduction are a detailed biography of the author, discussing major life events and important literary works. Then follows a thematic and structural analysis of the work, which traces significant themes, patterns, and motifs. An annotated list of characters supplies brief information on the chief characters in the work.

A selection of critical extracts, derived from previously published material by leading critics, then follows. The extracts consist of statements by the author, early reviews of the work, and later evaluations up to the present. These items are arranged chronologically by date of first publication. A bibliography of the author's writings (including a complete list of all books written, cowritten, edited, and translated), a list of additional books and articles on the author and the work, and an index of themes conclude the volume.

Harold Bloom is Sterling Professor of the Humanities at Yale University and Henry W. and Albert A. Berg Professor of English at the New York University Graduate School. He is the author of twenty books and the editor of more than thirty anthologies of literary criticism.

Professor Bloom's works include *Shelley's Mythmaking* (1959), *The Visionary Company* (1961), *Blake's Apocalypse* (1963), *Yeats* (1970), *A Map of Misreading* (1975), *Kabbalah and Criticism* (1975), and *Agon: Towards a Theory of Revisionism* (1982). *The Anxiety of Influence* (1973) sets forth Professor Bloom's provocative theory of the literary relationships between the great writers and their predecessors. His most recent books include *The American Religion* (1992), *The Western Canon* (1994), and *Omens of Millennium: The Gnosis of Angels, Dreams, and Resurrection* (1996).

Professor Bloom earned his Ph.D. from Yale University in 1955 and has served on the Yale faculty since then. He is a 1985 MacArthur Foundation Award recipient and served as the Charles Elkot Norton Professor of Poetry at Harvard University in 1987–88. He is currently the editor of other Chelsea House series in literary criticism, including MAJOR LITERARY CHARACTERS, MODERN CRITICAL VIEWS, and WOMEN WRITERS OF ENGLISH AND THEIR WORKS.

Editor's Note

My Introduction centers upon Caddy Compson and her relation to Faulkner's anxieties: cultural, literary, and personal. Critical Extracts commence with the French philosopher-novelist Jean-Paul Sartre, who sees the novel's world as one in which everything has already happened, and nothing new can ever come to be, and yet "the order of the past is the order of the heart."

John Arthos considers that Faulkner's vision of evil reduces to the world's invasion of the soul, while Ralph Ellison, author of the great novel *Invisible Man*, finds in Faulkner a mode of guilt in which black people symbolize the author's own personal rebellion.

Form in *The Sound and The Fury*'s four sections is discussed by Olga W. Vickery, who argues that Faulkner creates a tight structure while rendering the central situation ambiguous, a finding augmented by Frederick J. Hoffman's remarks upon perspective in the book's view of truth.

Peter Swiggart centers upon Jason Compson's brutal monologue, which reveals the viciousness of his decayed gentility, after which John W. Hunt centers upon the agony of Quentin Compson's "myopic moralism."

The major critic Cleanth Brooks traces the reader's progress in *The Sound and The Fury*, "from murkiness to increasing enlightenment," while Joseph Brogunier examines the influence of the poet A. E. Housman upon Faulkner's novel.

George C. Bedell criticizes Sartre for making no distinction between Faulkner and his characters, and John T. Irwin, the best of all Faulkner critics, traces in Quentin's suicide the need to drown his narcissistic shadow.

Andre Bleikosten examines failure as a creative obsession in *The Sound and The Fury*, while Lynn Gartrell Levins ascribes Quentin's suicide to his mother's failure in love.

Gary Lee Stonum sums up the book's technique as Faulkner's attempt to achieve a clearer focus on Caddy, while Warwick Wadlington sees Faulkner as attempting a tragedy bearing the mark of Sophocles.

Black-white relationships in *The Sound and The Fury* are the emphasis of Thadius M. Davis, while Gail L. Mortimer traces the problem of time in Quentin's monologue and Jessie McGuire Coffee meditates upon Benjy as a figure of sacrifice.

James M. Cox, a major scholar of American literature, discusses the image of loss in the novel, and Deborah Clark concludes the Critical Extracts by considering how shrewdly and obsessively Faulkner has written Caddy Compson out of his text.

Introduction

HAROLD BLOOM

Faulkner was immensely concerned with the tensions between fathers and sons, while he regarded female sexuality as being closely allied with death. His literary fathers included the American poets T. S. Eliot and Hart Crane, the Polish-British novelist Joseph Conrad, and the Irish epic writer James Joyce. All of them are reflected in *The Sound and The Fury,* which seems to me the principal arena where Faulkner attempts to resolve his anxieties of influence. It is also where a horror of families is allied to a quest for aesthetic dignity, and where both are represented by a link between incestuous jealousy and the fear of dying.

Caddy Compson is the center of *The Sound and The Fury,* a triumph of emotional nuance and metaphorical intensity even though she is never present to us in direct narration. Rather, Caddy is mediated by four narrators—her three brothers and Faulkner himself—who give us an Eliotic "heap of broken images," a figurative wealth of associations and attributes out of which we must reconstruct this southern young woman, a kind of universal Eve, though viewed as sister rather than mother.

Caddy is an unforgettable cluster of images: the odor of honeysuckle, the color red, pear trees, twilight, fire, and the river. Taken together, these intimate the ideal of southern womanhood, a nostalgia for the past, and a sense of loss that relates the sacrifice of virginity to death. From the ideological perspectives now current in our culture, some rightly regard Caddy Compson as a monument to male exploitation of the female. Indubitably, Caddy emerges from Faulkner's Jacobean misogyny, derived by him from Eliot's concern with the dramatists Cyril Tourneur, John Ford, and John Webster. As an image of social degradation founded upon an enigmatic idealization of women, Faulkner's Caddy becomes an Oedipal nightmare for her brother Quentin, who feels himself betrayed by her fall from a social code of supposed honor. Incest, as Shelly remarked, is the most poetic of all circumstances, and Caddy is one of the major American literary images of male desire for the forbidden (because related) female. Caddy is at once the emblem of her brother Quentin's suicide and also Faulkner's version of what Sigmund Freud called the Death Drive beyond the Pleasure Principle. You might term Caddy the Southern Twilight, a great image for the death of a southern myth.

I once wrote that it is because *The Sound and The Fury's* four-fold narrative has no defenses against Candace Compson that we are convinced we know her so well, even though we (and Faulkner) do not know her at all. In the appendix that he composed for Malcom Cowley's *The Portable Faulkner,* the novelist tried to sum up his absent heroine by emphasizing that her true desire was for her repressed and suicidal brother:

> Doomed and knew it; accepted doom without either seeking or fleeing it. Loved her brother despite him . . . she loved him in spite of but because of the fact that he himself was incapable of love.

Caddy's stoic fatalism is Faulkner's own: she is the perfect image of the novelist's yearning for the sister he never had. It is a curiosity of modern American literature that its most vividly haunting female protagonist is scarcely there upon the page at all. ✣

Biography of
William Faulkner
(1897–1962)

William Faulkner was born on September 25, 1897, in New Albany, Mississippi, to Murry and Maud Butler Falkner (the "u" was added to his name in error by a publisher in 1918; Faulkner adopted the spelling). The Falkner family had lived in northern Mississippi since before the Civil War. His mother, who was educated at the Women's College of Columbus, Mississippi, introduced William to classic literary works, ranging from William Shakespeare to Joseph Conrad. When William was five, his family moved to Oxford, Mississippi, where Murry Falkner held various jobs, including employment in a livery stable and a hardware store, to support his growing family. Faulkner would place nearly all of his novels in a fictional version of Oxford, which he named Jefferson.

To help manage William and his brothers, Murry, John, and Dean, the Falkners enlisted the aid of Maud Butler's mother, known to the boys as "Damuddy," and a black servant, Caroline Barr ("Mammy Callie"). The latter taught William how to tell stories, and at age nine, he decided he would be a writer. By the time he was a teenager, however, he had grown bored with school and began skipping classes so he could read medical textbooks. Although William dropped out of high school before his junior year, he taught himself French in order to read the Symbolist poets and he read widely in modern English literature.

In 1918, Faulkner tried to enlist for U.S. pilot training, but he was too short and too lightweight to be admitted into the armed services. Later that year, he joined Britain's Royal Air Force, completing his training after the November 11th armistice that ended World War I. Although he did not see combat, Faulkner nonetheless discarded his cadet's uniform and secured a full (and unearned) officer's uniform, complete with the wings of the Royal Flying Corps and the pips of a lieutenant. In America, he wore the uniform constantly, his story being that he had been wounded in France in a plane crash.

Faulkner attended the University of Mississippi for one year and then worked at various jobs in New York while he wrote. He contributed one poem to *New Republic* magazine and several drawings and poems to *The Mississippian*. His first book was a volume of poems, *The Marble Faun* (1924). During a six-month stay in New Orleans that year, Faulkner met short-story writer and novelist Sherwood Anderson, who would become his mentor. He then traveled to Europe, returning on the publication of his first novel, *Soldiers' Pay* (1926). His next novel, *Mosquitoes* (1927), based largely on the work of James Joyce and T. S. Eliot, was not as well received as his first, and *Flags in the Dust,* which was initially rejected, was revised into *Sartoris* (1929), the first of his Yoknapatawpha novels, named for the fictional county he introduced in this book. Faulkner continued to trace the county's inhabitants and history in *The Sound and the Fury* (1929). Faulkner said that he wrote this novel in an ecstasy of emotion; although he later dubbed it his "most magnificent failure," *The Sound and the Fury* earned critical praise and is considered one of his finest works.

In 1929, Faulkner married Estelle Oldham Franklin; they had one child, Jill (b. 1933). The following year, he published *As I Lay Dying,* which also received positive reviews but sold poorly. Early critical attention turned to notoriety with the publication of *Sanctuary* (1931); the novel's sensational subject matter won a sizable readership and attracted enough publicity to place Faulkner in high demand as a contributor to magazines.

Light in August (1932) and *Absalom, Absalom!* (1936) established Faulkner's literary reputation. In the 1940s he turned to scriptwriting in Hollywood as a means to make a living, having worked intermittently for MGM Studios since 1932. His publications during this period include *The Unvanquished* (1938); two short novels published together as *The Wild Palms* (1939); *The Hamlet* (1940), the first novel in the "Snopes" trilogy; and

Go Down, Moses (1942). In 1939, he was elected into the National Institute of Arts and Letters.

Faulkner's second rise to fame began in 1946 with the publication of *The Portable Faulkner*, edited by Malcolm Cowley. He published *Intruder in the Dust*, his first popular success after *Sanctuary*, in 1948. His *Collected Stories* (1950) won him a National Book Award, and the same year he won the Nobel Prize for Literature for 1949, delivering an acceptance speech in Stockholm which has become famous.

Now a public figure, he traveled abroad for the State Department, visiting South America in 1954 and 1961, Asia in 1955, and Europe in 1955 and 1957. From 1957 to 1958 he was writer in residence at the University of Virginia. He was awarded the Pulitzer Prize twice, for *The Town* (1957) and *The Reivers* (1962). Faulkner died of a heart attack in Byhalia, Mississippi, on July 6, 1962. ✤

Thematic and Structural Analysis

The title of Faulkner's *The Sound and the Fury* is taken from Shakespeare's Macbeth, during the scene where Macbeth hears of his wife's death. He cries out:

> Tomorrow, and tomorrow, and tomorrow
> Creeps in this petty pace from day to day,
> To the last syllable of recorded time;
> And all our yesterdays have lighted fools
> The way to dusty death. Out, out, brief candle!
> Life's but a walking shadow, a poor player
> That struts and frets his hour upon the stage
> And then is heard no more: it is a tale
> Told by an idiot, full of sound and fury
> Signifying nothing. (*Macbeth* 5.5)

The significance of the novel's title is easily recognized in Benjy, the 33-year-old idiot child of the Compson family, through whose eyes the first section is presented. However, the title also refers to the meaning of the novel itself and to its unusual structure. The idea that life is a shadow occurs several times throughout the book, especially in the section about Quentin Compson. Quentin also views blacks as "obverse reflection[s]" of white people; Benjy perceives the world as light and shadow, as disconnected images. Moreover, Faulkner's tale is filled with sounds—Benjy's moaning, the cries of mourners, Quentin's watch ticking, Dilsey singing—and with fury—Jason's rage at his family and toward strangers, for example.

Other themes in the novel are death and loss, and the passage of time. The novel contains four deaths (that of Damuddy, Quentin, Mr. Compson, and Dilsey's husband, Roskus) and much of the book is devoted to the other characters' reactions to their losses and to the disintegration of the Compson family. Faulkner also shifts the concept of time with each section of the book. Throughout the novel, in varying degrees, the past invades the present and the future is either nonexistent or in jeopardy.

Faulkner arranged *The Sound and the Fury* into four sections named by specific, nonchronological dates. The first three sections, **April Seventh, 1928; June Second, 1910;** and **April Sixth, 1928** are stream-of-consciousness narratives that take place in the minds of three members of the Compson family: Benjy, Quentin, and Jason IV, respectively, the sons of Caroline and Jason Compson III. The fourth section, **April Eighth, 1928**, is a straightforward account by an omniscient narrator centering on Dilsey, the Compson's black servant and the novel's most stable figure.

Each section varies stylistically according to the nature of the character who is narrating; that is, the character in whose mind Faulkner wishes the reader to reside. (For purposes of clarity in this discussion, the sections are named for these characters, although Faulkner does not distinguish them in this way.) In the **Benjy section (April Seventh, 1928)**, the narrative style is disjointed and unreflective to represent the thoughts of a mentally handicapped adult. Faulkner presents a series of unconnected sensory images, set in simple vocabulary and linked by Benjy's seemingly arbitrary mental associations. For example, the sound of golfers crying "caddie" at the golf course near the Compson home triggers a memory of Benjy's sister, Caddy.

In the **Quentin section (June Second, 1910)**, the narrator's mind also returns continually to the past. But where Benjy experiences reality only through sensory impressions, Quentin examines the motivations and the consequences of every action, past and present. Thus, the sentence structure and vocabulary of the **Quentin section** are much more complex than that of the **Benjy section**.

While the pace of the **Quentin section** is ponderous and the thoughts extremely detailed, the **Jason section (April Sixth, 1928)** moves swiftly, just as the character himself—a selfish, mean-spirited man—rushes from place to place, unconcerned with moral intricacies and consequences. Finally, the **Dilsey section (April Eighth, 1928)**, narrated by the author, is quiet

and dignified in style and contains images of order, peaceful-
ness, and control.

The events of *The Sound and the Fury* span 30 years, from
1898 to 1928. Throughout the novel, recurring events from this
period are presented as they are perceived by the narrators.
Among the most significant are the death of Damuddy, the
Compson children's grandmother (1898), the changing of
Benjy's name (1900), Christmas (1902), Caddy's period of
sexual maturation (1905-1910), Caddy's wedding (1910),
Quentin's suicide (1910), Mr. Compson's death (1912), Benjy's
castration (1913), and the present (1928). Faulkner signals time
shifts in two ways: by using italic type, as he will also do in the
Quentin section (although longer scenes usually revert to
Roman type), and by mentioning one of Benjy's three succes-
sive caretakers, Versh, T. P., or Luster.

The novel begins in the present on April 7, 1928. It is Holy
Saturday and Benjy's 33rd birthday—a symbolic link to
Christ, who was crucified at the same age. Running along the
fence surrounding the Compson home, Benjy follows the
players on the nearby golf course while his 14-year-old attendant, Luster, searches for a lost quarter that he needs to pay
for a show that evening.

Luster guides Benjy through a hole in the fence and Benjy
gets snagged on a nail. This reminds him of a similar episode
that occurred on December 23, 1902, when Caddy took him
on an errand and they climbed under a fence. She tells Benjy
to keep his hands in his pockets so they will not get cold. Earlier that day, Benjy's attendant, Versh, had also warned him
about his hands while they were preparing to meet Caddy on
her way home from school. Benjy recalls that Caddy "smelled
like trees." Throughout the remainder of the section, Benjy's
mind will flicker in the present before returning to events of
the past.

As Benjy and Luster pass the carriage house, Benjy sees a
new wheel on the carriage, which reminds him of a day in
1912 when he went to the cemetery with his mother to visit
the graves of his father and his brother Quentin. After a brief

return to the present, he again recalls December 23, 1902, when he and Caddy went on an errand to deliver Maury Bascomb's letter to Mrs. Patterson, then to an earlier, unspecified time when he was delivering a message alone and Mr. Patterson intercepted it.

Luster leads Benjy to the branch (or creek) to look for the quarter. A golf ball lands nearby and Luster pockets it, hoping that he can sell it. When Benjy steps into the branch, he relives fragments about another important day in the novel: the day of Damuddy's death in 1898. Attended by Versh, Benjy (then called Maury) is playing in the same branch with Quentin, Jason, and Caddy. Quentin slaps Caddy for removing her wet dress and she falls in the branch and muddies her drawers, then threatens to run away if she is punished. Maury begins crying and Caddy consoles him.

Roskus calls the children to supper. Caddy and Quentin try to bribe Jason not to tell about their water fight, and Quentin hopes that if they walk slowly it will soon be too dark for his parents to see Caddy's muddy drawers. Versh carries Maury up the hill.

As they near the house, they see Roskus milking a cow. This sight makes Benjy remember the day of Caddy's wedding, April 25, 1910, when T. P., his second caretaker, gets them both drunk on "sassprilluh" and lets the cows out of the barn. Quentin repeatedly hits T. P. in an attempt to sober him up. Benjy falls down repeatedly and vomits; Quentin and Versh carry him to the barn.

In 1898 again, all but Quentin head home for dinner. Caddy and Versh discuss whether the Compsons have company, since the house is brightly lit. Jason lags behind and because he keeps his hands in his pockets, he keeps falling down. When they reach the house, Jason immediately tells on Caddy, but Mr. Compson scarcely reacts. Instead, he instructs the children to stay with Dilsey, and at Caddy's insistence puts her "in charge" of the other children.

The branch episode in *The Sound and the Fury* is widely believed to be a microcosmic view of the main characters and their fates. Caddy falling down and getting her drawers muddy suggests her later promiscuity and her fall from the family's graces. Quentin's exaggerated concern for Caddy's welfare above his own foreshadows his inability to keep her "pure" and his subsequent despair and suicide. Jason's insularity and his habit of keeping his hands in his pockets symbolize the adult Jason's antisocial nature and his acquisitiveness. Benjy's sensitivity to Caddy's words and to departures from what he perceives as normal are evident later, when the adolescent Caddy has her first sexual experiences and he tries to force her into the bathroom to wash her clean.

While the children are eating supper, they hear sounds from another part of the house. Benjy begins to moan. Caddy says her mother is singing, but Quentin correctly identifies the sound as grieving. Jason begins to cry because he can no longer sleep with Damuddy. Interwoven with this scene are other images of death and corruption—buzzards, dead farm animals, decay—that symbolize the ultimate fate of the Compson family.

Instead of obeying Dilsey and going to bed after dinner, the children—except Quentin, who goes off alone—go to Versh's house. They see T. P. in front of the fire; the image reminds Benjy of a night in 1913 when he stayed at Dilsey's house all night and T. P. took him to the barn to watch Roskus milk the cows. Roskus orders T. P. to finish the milking and declares, "Taint no luck on this place."

Roskus's words trigger a memory of a time in 1910 when the black servant used similar words to describe the doomed Compson family, declaring that 15-year-old Benjy was one of the three signs of the family's demise. This is **June Second, 1910**, the night of Quentin's suicide, which the reader will see through Quentin's eyes in the next section.

Thinking of the time when he slept in T. P.'s bed, Benjy remembers a day in 1912 or 1913 when T. P. is helping Roskus with chores and Luster and young Quentin are playing together. "That's three, thank the Lawd," says Roskus, referring to the death of a third family member, Mr. Compson. Roskus declares that no luck can come to a family that forbids a child to hear the name of its mother (we later learn that Caddy his disgraced the family and that young Quentin is her child; Mrs. Compson will not allow Caddy's name to be spoken). Dilsey and her family discuss Benjy's intuitive knowledge of death.

After a brief memory of his father's body passing the house in a hearse, Benjy again recalls the night of Damuddy's death and then shifts several times to Dilsey moaning when Roskus dies (some time after the death of Mr. Compson). Though the children finally learn that Damuddy has died, Caddy insists that the gathering in the main house is a party, not a funeral.

Benjy returns to 1910, the night that the Compsons hear of Quentin's suicide. "I could smell it," he recalls, alluding to his uncanny awareness of death, and he begins to moan loudly. T. P. takes him to the pasture, where he can bellow without disturbing anyone else. Benjy howls while watching the buzzards picking at the remains of a farm animal. This triggers his memory of Caddy wondering whether Damuddy would also be "undressed" by buzzards.

Caddy decides to see whether there is a party in the house, and she climbs a tree outside the parlor window. Below her, the other children can see her muddy drawers. Dilsey comes out and lifts Caddy out of the tree, telling Versh to find Quentin. They go inside and encounter their father, whose expression makes them silent. Breaking routine, Dilsey leads the children to the room where they slept when they had measles. Jason cries because he cannot sleep with Damuddy. Quentin comes in weeping, his face turned away. When Caddy removes her dress, Dilsey notices her muddy drawers, strips her, and tries to scrub her clean. The children lie down—Quentin facing the wall and Caddy beside Maury. Maury begins to dream.

Interspersed with the memories of Damuddy's death are scenes from Caddy's wedding day in 1910—less than two months before Quentin's suicide—when Benjy catches glimpses of his sister wearing flowers in her hair and "a long veil like shining wind." In both episodes, Benjy is given "sassprilluh" to drink and peeks through the window to view the action in the house. The shift from funeral to wedding scene illustrates how Faulkner connects death and sexuality throughout the novel.

In the wedding scenes, Benjy notes that Caddy no longer smells like trees. Faulkner uses this association repeatedly to signal Caddy's sexual maturity. For example, Benjy also recalls a time in 1906 when Caddy does not smell like trees—she is 14 years old and has just begun using perfume. She eventually realizes that the strange scent upsets Benjy, and she washes it off and gives the bottle of perfume to Dilsey. When Caddy smells like trees again, Benjy is happy.

Because Caddy is able to "wash away" this first departure from Benjy's normal experience of her, he will try on other occasions to do the same by forcing her into the bathroom. This occurs after Caddy has been on the porch swing kissing a suitor and after she loses her virginity. The theme of washing away one's sins will recur most significantly in the **Quentin section**, when Caddy lies in the branch up to her hips after losing her virginity, and in the **Dilsey section**, with the early morning rain and the churchgoers being washed "in the blood of the Lamb."

Benjy's memory of 14-year-old Caddy reminds him briefly of a time (around 1908) when he was 13 years old. He was told that he was too big to sleep with Caddy any more and is brought to Uncle Maury's room instead. He remembers that his uncle's "eye was sick, and his mouth"—he had been attacked by Mr. Patterson, the husband of the woman with whom he was having an affair. Mr. Compson ridicules his brother-in-law, and Mrs. Compson complains he doesn't think her family is as good as his. Benjy stops crying only when Caddy lies down with him in Uncle Maury's room.

Without transition, Benjy returns to 1898, when Caddy is in the tree looking into the house. All she sees are people "sitting in chairs and looking." This memory reminds Benjy of another time when T. P. left him and he went off toward the kitchen to find Caddy. In the present, Luster returns from finding his golf ball and tries to keep Benjy from wandering over to the porch, where Miss Quentin is sitting with her boyfriend, a man wearing a red tie. He remembers going to the swing and crying on Caddy's wedding day, and then in 1906 or 1907 when Caddy was in the swing with her boyfriend, Charlie.

Upon seeing Caddy with a man, Benjy howls and Caddy jumps down to hold him. Annoyed, Charlie continues to try and embrace her, assuring her that Benjy can't talk and so he won't tell. Caddy replies that he can see what is happening, just as he sensed Damuddy's death. She brings Benjy back into the house and begins to cry, promising Benjy that she "won't anymore." She washes her mouth with soap.

In the present, Miss Quentin sees Benjy approaching the porch; he is moaning because he is thinking of Caddy. Miss Quentin threatens to have Dilsey whip Luster for letting Benjy follow her around and accuses them of being spies for her grandmother, Mrs. Compson. We learn that the man in a red tie is with the traveling show in town for the weekend. He viciously teases Benjy, and Miss Quentin angrily runs off to tell Dilsey; the man thinks she is upset because he is bothering Benjy. Luster, still concerned with finding his quarter, tries to sell the golf ball to the man. They find a box of prophylactics that one of Miss Quentin's other boyfriends left there, and Luster says that "they comes every night she can climb down that tree."

Luster takes Benjy along the fence to the front gate. The gate scenes that follow present Benjy as innocent but sexually mature and therefore threatening. One day in 1910, after Caddy has married and left the house, he waits by the front gate, thinking that Caddy will eventually come back. On another occasion that same year, Benjy sees a group of girls passing by and runs along the fence after them, trying to tell them about Caddy. Finally, he recalls his father and Jason discussing whether he should be committed to an asylum.

This scene follows another incident when the gate, usually locked, was left open. Benjy follows a group of girls passing by and seizes one girl, "trying to say" how much he misses Caddy. The girl becomes frightened and screams, and Benjy is attacked with a fence post by the girl's father. He falls down the hill.

As a result of this incident, Benjy is castrated. Jason and his father fear that sexual urges may have triggered Benjy's pursuit of the girls. They do not understand that he associates the gate and the young girls with Caddy.

The remainder of the **Benjy section** shifts rapidly from 1900 to 1928, with brief references to 1898 and two recollections from 1910 when Caddy loses her virginity. Although 1928 is chronologically the present, Benjy's mind seems to operate in 1900, only fleetingly returning to the present.

Exasperated over Benjy's moaning, Luster tells him that he will be committed to an asylum when Mrs. Compson dies. He takes his flowers and whispers "Caddy" until Benjy begins to bellow. Dilsey calls them inside to light the candles on Benjy's birthday cake.

The scenes that follow are linked by images of fire, rain, and reflections. While Benjy watches the fire in the stove, he remembers seeing another fire on the day that his mother changed his name. Annoyed that the three-year-old is not listening, she instructs Caddy to take away his special pillow. When he begins to moan, Mrs. Compson collapses and Caddy takes Benjy away, telling her mother to go upstairs so she "can be sick." Brief thoughts of this day will be interwoven throughout this part of the section.

Dilsey lights the candles on Benjy's birthday cake and tells Benjy and Luster to eat it before Jason sees it and makes a fuss about the expense (Dilsey has purchased the cake with her own money). Luster blows out the candles and Benjy cries because the flames are gone. Luster opens the stove door. In 1910 it is raining, a fire is lit in the room, and Benjy hears a clock ticking and Caddy crying.

Luster teases Benjy by opening and closing the oven door with a wire. Briefly, Benjy remembers Caddy explaining to Dilsey why his name was changed. While Dilsey is scolding Luster, Benjy reaches into the fire, burns his hand, and howls. Dilsey administers to his injury and sends Luster to fetch an old slipper of Caddy's, which soothes Benjy, and sends the two to the library. Hearing the noise, Mrs. Compson comes downstairs, accuses the servants of deliberately trying to annoy her, and complains about the "cheap store cake" Dilsey bought.

This passage illuminates the vast difference between the self-centered Mrs. Compson, who succeeds only in upsetting Benjy, and the maternal natures of Dilsey and Caddy, who are the only characters in *The Sound and the Fury* who seem almost instinctively to understand Benjy's reactions. In scenes from 1898 and 1900, it is Caddy, not Mrs. Compson, who is the maternal figure, carrying Benjy upstairs after playing in the branch and letting him have his special cushion and sit by the fire.

In 1900, Benjy watches Caddy and Jason fighting. After Caddy sends her mother upstairs, she accuses Jason of destroying Benjy's paper dolls and attacks him. Mr. Compson, who "smells like rain," tries to separate them. Quentin enters the library, also smelling like rain, and Caddy tells him about the paper dolls. She notices that Quentin has been in a fight. His father also notices and asks him about the fight. Jason is crying in another part of the room and his father tells him to stop. Dilsey announces supper; Versh carries Benjy to the table and discusses his new name. Benjy notices that Versh, too, smells like rain. Caddy feeds Benjy, then takes him to the library to sit on his favorite cushion while he looks at the mirror and the fire.

Now Benjy remembers when Caddy comes in the house and walks quickly past the door (it is 1910). Mrs. Compson calls to her. Caddy glances at Benjy, who senses a change in her and starts to cry. He tries to go to Caddy, who also begins crying and backs away from him several times. When he sees her eyes he cries even louder and pulls at her dress. He follows her upstairs and tries to push her into the bathroom to wash, as he has done before. But Caddy, who has lost her virginity, knows that she cannot wash it away this time and so she avoids Benjy. This change will ultimately separate them.

Alternating every few lines with the dinner scene of 1900 is another dinner in the present. Benjy and Luster are in the library when Jason enters; he and Luster complain about Benjy. Dilsey announces supper and asks about Miss Quentin. Luster asks Jason for a quarter to attend the show that night, and Jason—who has already burned two free passes to the show—refuses. Miss Quentin enters to see whether Dilsey has announced supper.

At the table, Miss Quentin says that Benjy should take Caddy's old slipper and eat in the kitchen. "It's like eating with a pig," she comments. Jason and Miss Quentin get into a fierce argument about her seeing the show man. Miss Quentin accuses them all of spying on her and threatens to run away. She tries to throw a glass of water at Jason; Dilsey tries to calm her and is rebuffed. Miss Quentin runs upstairs.

Later, Benjy is sitting in a dark room of the house holding the slipper. Luster finds him and announces that Miss Quentin has given him a quarter to see the show. As Luster prepares him for bed, Benjy remembers the night of Damuddy's death and sleeping in a different room. Mrs. Compson locks the door to Miss Quentin's room after checking to see that she is in it. After he is undressed, Benjy sees himself in the mirror, remembers his castration, and begins to cry. "Looking for them ain't going to do no good," Luster remarks. "They're gone." Luster and Benjy watch through the window as Miss Quentin climbs out of her bedroom window and down the tree by the house. (We will learn in the **Dilsey section** that she has run away with the man in the red tie after stealing thousands of dollars from Jason.)

The **Benjy section** ends on the night of Damuddy's death in 1898. Dilsey puts the children to bed in the "measles" room; she scolds Caddy for her muddy drawers and threatens to whip Jason if he doesn't stop whining. Caddy asks her father if Mother is sick, and he asks her to take care of Maury. Maury falls asleep beside Caddy.

If Benjy is incapable of distinguishing between past and present, his suicidal brother, Quentin, who narrates the second section of the novel (**June Second, 1910**), is obsessed with time. On the last day of his life, Quentin Compson is fixated on two subjects: his failure to preserve Caddy's innocence and his father's nihilistic view that life is valueless. Time cures all, Mr. Compson dispassionately has told his son, but Quentin does not want to believe it. If this is true, he reasons, then the pain he feels over Caddy's sins has no meaning and his own values are worthless. Since he cannot live without a set of principles governing his life, he begins to feel that taking his life is the only way to stop time.

As in the **Benjy section**, Faulkner applies a stream-of-consciousness technique to the **Quentin section**. The present is interrupted by memories from past events in the lives of the

Compsons. Here, however, we experience the thoughts of a reasoning and intelligent mind bogged down with complex and difficult ideas and contemplating suicide; therefore, the sentence structure and language are also complex. The sound of the ticking watch in the opening scene, for example, leads Quentin to think about the source of the watch (his father) and to recall his father's words upon giving it to him (that one cannot conquer time and that "victory is an illusion of philosophers and fools"). And where Benjy is incapable of distinguishing the past from the present, Quentin struggles to understand the effects of past events on the future of his family.

The passage of time and Quentin's attempts to escape or stop it are the predominant themes in the **Quentin section**. In the opening scene, he wakes up in his dormitory room and immediately determines the time of day by the shadow of the sash at the window. "I was in time again," he says, "hearing the watch." One of the first things he does is to break the crystal and twist the hands off his ticking watch—an unbearable reminder of time moving. Yet the watch continues to operate, its "little wheels clicking and clicking" behind its face, "not knowing any better."

Throughout the day, Quentin will repeatedly ask about the time, even though he is trying to escape it. This is consistent with his belief in the necessity of stopping time: that the watches in the jeweler's window contradict one another, for example, signifies a partial defeat or a "slowing" of time to him.

Another significant theme of the **Quentin section** is that of water, a recurring motif in *The Sound and the Fury*. For Quentin, water represents both purification and death. One of Quentin's strongest recollections is that of Caddy sitting in the branch after she has lost her virginity, letting the water run over her hips. But water is also the means by which Quentin takes his own life, drowning himself in a river. In this way, Faulkner also emphasizes another theme, the connection between sex and death. Mr. Compson tells Quentin that female virginity is a negative state "like death." Quentin himself alludes to "the good Saint Francis who said Little Sister Death, that never had a sister." Quentin's roommate Shreve notices his formal dress and asks, "Is it a wedding or a wake?" Caddy says of her many sexual partners, "When they touched me I died." And Quentin's thoughts continually return to the day of Damuddy's death and the sight of Caddy's muddy drawers—which were made so when Quentin himself pushed her into the water. This scene resonates in the later branch scene with Caddy, when Quentin suggests incest or double suicide as means to unite them against their family and the rest of the world.

Quentin hears the bedsprings of his roommate, Shreve, and then his slippers scuffing across the floor, and recalls other comments his father has made about time. This in turn reminds him of Caddy's wedding day and of his attempt to tell his father that he committed incest with her. He thinks of being teased by classmates about his virginity—they call Shreve his husband. "In the South you are ashamed of being a virgin," he thinks. "Boys. Men. They lie about it. Because it means less to women, Father said. He said it was men invented virginity not women." Quentin remembers asking his father why it could not have been him and not Caddy who is "unvirgin"; his father replies that it is not even worth contemplating, since virginity is not a virtue anyway.

Quentin looks out the window and sees Spoade, a fellow student from the South. He is reminded of Caddy's boyfriend Dalton Ames and of his father's reaction to his attempts to tell him that it was he, not Ames, who seduced Caddy. "[P]eople cannot do anything that dreadful," his father replies, and worse, they are unable to remember from one day to the next what they originally perceived as dreadful. With this thought in mind, Quentin begins contemplating suicide. He tries to destroy his watch, but succeeds only in removing the hands and sustaining a minor cut on his thumb, which he treats.

Next, Quentin packs his clothing in a trunk and addresses it, presumably to his parents. He dresses in a new suit, packs the rest of his belongings, drops the trunk key in an envelope addressed to his father, and writes two suicide notes to Shreve. He thinks of Caddy in her wedding dress and of Benjy's bellowing while T. P. drank sassprilluh on the day of the wedding.

Quentin stops at the post office before breakfast to mail the envelope addressed to his father. He puts the letters to Shreve in his pocket. The whole time that Quentin is making these preparations, he is constantly aware of the sounds of clocks and watches and of the progression of shadows.

After breakfast Quentin enters a jeweler's shop, shows the jeweler his watch, and asks whether any of the watches in the window show the correct time. When the jeweler tries to tell him the time, he says that he doesn't want to know—he only needs to know whether the watches are right. He leaves the jeweler's without having his watch repaired. He is pleased to find that the watches in the window show different times, "with the same assertive and contradictory assurance" that his watch had. He remembers his father's statement that time comes alive only when clocks stop.

Quentin enters a hardware store and buys two six-pound flatirons, which he will use to weight himself down when he jumps off the bridge. He boards a streetcar and sits beside a black man, whose presence reminds him that he misses Dilsey and Roskus. He slips into reverie about the way he counted time as a schoolchild and about Benjy's ability to sense change and his ignorance of time passing, even when his name was changed.

Quentin gets off the streetcar near a bridge and watches his shadow in the river, thinking that he had tricked it and "it would not quit" him, remembering that blacks believe that "a drowned man's shadow was watching for him in the water all the time." He sees a shell (or boat) being carried into the river and thinks of Gerald Bland, another student. Bland is a womanizer who believes that all women are "bitches," and Quentin again thinks of Dalton Ames and his father, both of whom hold the same opinion. Neither Bland nor Ames have sisters.

Quentin briefly returns to the present after hearing his watch and feeling the letters in his pocket, then thinks of Caddy, particularly of her sexual exploits and the first time he meets her fiancé, Herbert Head. Herbert purchased a car for Caddy—the first to be seen in Jefferson—and has promised a bank job to Jason. Quentin recalls his mother's selfish pride in Jason and her belief that he was the only Compson to take after her side of the family. He boards another streetcar.

Interwoven with these thoughts are brief, fragmented memories of Caddy's wedding. He also thinks about the sale of Benjy's pasture to fund his college education and then about his mother telling him that she wants Herbert and Quentin to be more than friends; this in turn reminds him of his attempted confession of incest. He concludes that Mrs. Compson was incapable of fulfilling her role as mother to her children—If I could say Mother. Mother," he thinks. While Mrs. Compson and Herbert talk, Quentin looks at Caddy, who averts her eyes. Another time, Mrs. Compson objects to people spying on Caddy and claims that her husband has taught their children to disrespect her; Mr. Compson tells Quentin that women are inherently suspicious and evil.

Quentin gives one of the letters he is carrying to a black man named Deacon, instructing him to deliver it to Shreve the following day. Deacon promises to do so. He hears chimes again and remembers several scenes from his childhood; he meets Shreve coming toward him and tells him that Deacon has a note for him. Shreve asks what Quentin has under his arm (the weights) and he tells him it is a pair of shoes. Shreve tells Quentin that he has received a note from Mrs. Bland.

The mention of Gerald's mother reminds Quentin of his own mother. She wanted to take Jason—the only child she loves—away from the rest of the family to save him from the family "curse." She feels disgraced not only by Benjy's incapacity, but also by her daughter's promiscuity, which she views as a lack of regard for her own honor.

Quentin thinks of his father's philosophy that "man is the sum of his misfortunes." He again becomes aware of his watch ticking and gets off the streetcar to walk along a nearby river. The river reminds him of Gerald Bland, who in turn reminds him of Dalton Ames, Caddy's disgrace, and Caddy's request that he take care of Benjy and Mr. Compson after her departure from the Compson house. He recalls that Mrs. Bland, who was concerned about his social status, once decided to find Quentin a new roommate and ordered him to have Shreve move out.

While Quentin struggles with these thoughts, he also recalls his first private meeting with Herbert Head in the Compson library. He is aware that Herbert has cheated, he tells him, and he will not tell his parents. Herbert casually replies that cheating is not illegal or sinful and that he simply happened to get caught. Herbert offers money to Quentin, who is deeply offended. Their argument escalates until Caddy enters the room. She sends Herbert away so that she can talk to Quentin, and then tells Quentin to keep out of her affairs.

Quentin sees that Caddy is sick and she admits it, but won't tell him how. Quentin insists that if she's sick she can't marry, and Caddy replies, "I've got to marry somebody." This is the reader's first clue that Caddy is already pregnant. Quentin asks her how many men she has slept with; she tells him that she doesn't know, and therefore does not know who the father of her child is.

Quentin is now walking along the "swooping curve" of the river and "tramping [his] shadow into the dust." He can "feel" the water (much like Benjy feels change); when he reaches the bridge he sits and watches the river as it hits the stones, noticing the bridge's shadow on the water. He hides the flatirons under the bridge. Throughout this scene, he is thinking about rising out of the water, about how his plunge into the river will redeem him, and about Christ's resurrection—a link to the rest of the novel, which takes place over Easter weekend, 1928. He wishes that his admission of incest with Caddy would banish them to a private hell, where he would have her all to himself and where "the clean flame" would absolve them of their sins.

The sound of a train whistle reminds Quentin of the voice of a black man named Louis Hatcher, who made a similar noise when he called his hunting dogs. This reminds him of Versh's tale about a man who mutilated himself with a razor; he thinks that perhaps this is what Caddy is doing to herself morally. But then he remembers his father's assertion that virginity and purity are negative states and so they are contrary to nature. "It's nature is hurting you not Caddy," his father tells him.

While leaning on the rail of the bridge, Quentin sees three boys who are trying to win a $25 prize by catching an enormous trout. They discuss what they would do with the prize money. He asks the boys how far it is to the nearest town and whether there are any factories in town, for he hasn't heard the one o'clock whistle blow and he has broken his watch. They tell him where the nearest clock tower is, and he walks in that direction before sitting by the road.

The boys pass by; they haven't caught the fish. They point out the clock tower once again, then argue about whether to go swimming. Quentin tries to convince one boy to go swimming with his friends. This scene is one of several in which Faulkner underscores Quentin's constant desire to help others who may not need or ask for his help, just as his concern for Caddy's sins and for her welfare overshadow all other problems.

While the boys argue, Quentin's thoughts return to his discussion with Caddy in the library. He asks her to tell their father why she must marry, and then tells her that Herbert Head was expelled from school for cheating at cards and on a midterm. She replies that she's not going to play cards with him and asks him to take care of Mr. Compson and Benjy. She believes that their father will be dead in a year from drinking but that he is unable to stop, and fears that after his death, the other family members will have Benjy committed. Quentin remembers Benjy bellowing and pulling at Caddy's dress on the day she lost her virginity.

Quentin walks into town, noticing the "stupid assertion of the clock" in the distance. He enters a bakery, where he notices a small, dirty, Italian girl standing in front of the counter. He orders an extra sweet roll for her and takes her to a nearby drugstore for ice cream. When they leave, he asks where she lives, then suggests that she head home. When he turns around, he sees that she is following him.

Although Quentin repeatedly questions the girl about where she lives and makes several attempts to guide her home, she continues to follow him, saying nothing. Finally, he gives her a quarter and runs away, but when he looks again she is coming up the road. By now they are out of town and heading for the country. She continues to follow him and he grows increasingly bothered, until finally he decides to return to town to get rid of her. Along the way, they encounter the three boys again, who are now swimming. They are naked and demand that Quentin take the girl away. Quentin feels sorry for the child, since she is "just a girl."

As Quentin searches for the girl's home, he thinks constantly of Caddy. He recalls how he slapped her because she made a man kiss her, and how she taunted him about his first sexual encounter with a girl named Natalie, whom Caddy thought was "dirty." He tells Caddy that he was hugging Natalie; Caddy says she doesn't care. Quentin replies that he'll make her care and smears her with mud; they fight. It is raining; they lie down in the grass, both muddy. Caddy has scratched Quentin and he is bleeding; she suggests they wash themselves in the branch.

This scene reveals that Quentin's jealousy over Caddy's sexual partners is reciprocated by Caddy. Caddy is once again muddied by Quentin, suggesting that he is partly responsible for her sexual escapades. Faulkner uses the images of mud, blood, and washing to suggest sexuality.

As he heads toward town with the little girl, Quentin sees two men and a boy running toward him. The young man (named Julio) attacks Quentin, but the older man, who is the sheriff, pulls him off. Quentin learns that he is being accused of kidnapping or molesting the girl and is being taken to the town courthouse. Along the way, he encounters Mrs. Bland with Gerald, Spoade, Shreve, and two girls. He apologizes to Mrs. Bland for not getting her note and explains that he is under arrest. They try without success to have him released.

The judge hears Quentin's explanation and orders him to pay Julio one dollar and the court six dollars before he is dismissed. In the car with Mrs. Bland and the others, Quentin explains what happened. Then, as Mrs. Bland discusses wine and picnics, his mind wanders to thoughts of his childhood.

When he is arrested, Quentin realizes the absurdity of his situation. Throughout the day, he has been thinking about his father's opinion of women and of Bland's and Ames's assertion that they are all bitches. But when he himself tries to be kind to a small girl, he is accused of molesting her. On a more significant level, he has perhaps the same relationship with Caddy.

At this point in the **Quentin section** the present fades almost completely into the background as Quentin is consumed by thoughts of Caddy's promiscuity. He thinks of the night that she lost her virginity, when Benjy began howling and trying to force her into the bathroom and she ran out of the house and sat in the branch, letting the water run over her hips. Quentin finds her there and leads her to the bank. He asks whether she loves the man she has been with and whether he forced her to have sex; she replies no to both questions. She asks Quentin whether he has had any sexual experience. He says that he has, with "lots of girls," but she knows that he is lying and that he is a virgin.

Quentin tells her about his plan to admit to Mr. Compson that they had committed incest, telling Caddy that "it was me . . . I fooled you all the time it was me." He associates the scent of honeysuckle with Caddy because of the honeysuckle bush near the Compson porch, where she met many of her lovers.

Quentin begins to cry and reminds Caddy of the day Damuddy died and she got her drawers muddy. He puts a knife to her throat and suggests that he first kill her, then himself. Caddy agrees, and in a scene filled with language that strikingly links the themes of sex and death, Quentin tries to cut her throat. He is unable to follow through, however, and he drops the knife.

On the way back to the house, they meet one of Caddy's lovers. She introduces him, and Quentin walks off into the woods and lies down on the riverbank. Caddy finds him and he tells her to go home. Back at the house, Caddy tells Quentin that she believes the whole family is cursed, and he begins to cry. This memory blends into another one in which Quentin threatens to kill Dalton Ames if he does not leave town. Ames overpowers Quentin, who apparently faints. Caddy finds them and they begin arguing about Ames. Quentin forces Caddy to say his name.

Suddenly, Quentin returns to the present to discover Shreve and Spoade cleaning blood off of him. In thinking of Dalton

Ames, whose comments about women remind him of Gerald, he has attacked Gerald and been soundly beaten. He worries about getting blood on his good clothes and whether he should apologize to Bland. Shreve tells him to forget about both and wants to return to the school to get clean clothes for Quentin. Quentin says that he is not going back to town and tells Shreve that he will see him tomorrow.

It is now twilight, and Quentin is on another streetcar. He becomes keenly aware of the flickering of light and shadow around him. He smells "summer and darkness" and thinks again of the smell of honeysuckle, "the saddest odor of all." The trolley passes the river, and the reflections on its surface remind him of Benjy's love for mirrors. He changes cars, and this one crosses the bridge, "arching slow and high into space, between silence and nothingness."

On the way to his dormitory room, Quentin realizes that he can still hear his watch and notices that the chimes in the quad are sounding. He cleans the blood off his clothes with gasoline. The gas hurts his injured finger and reminds him of the smell of camphor, which his mother always used. He thinks of Caddy's car, of Dalton Ames on the bridge, and of the bridge where he concealed the flatirons.

As Quentin nears the end of his life, his thoughts become more disordered and his actions more ordered. In his mind his physical senses merge with one another: his nose can "see" the gasoline, eyes are "clenched like teeth," hands can see. Yet all the while, he is concerned about his clothing and personal hygiene.

The three-quarters chime sounds. "A quarter hour yet," he thinks, "And then I'll not be." His father had told him that mankind is worthless, that people are dolls "stuffed with saw-dust swept up from the trash heaps where all previous dolls had been thrown away." He remembers his father's cynical reaction to his tale of incest. Mr. Compson advised him to return to school and perhaps take a vacation.

As the last note of the chimes sounds, Quentin puts his good suit on again and is about to leave when he remembers he hasn't brushed his teeth or his hat. He takes care of both chores, borrowing Shreve's hatbrush so that he "didn't have to open the bag anymore."

"Once a bitch always a bitch," begins the **Jason section** (**April Sixth, 1928**), immediately indicating the vast difference in personality between Quentin Compson and his brother, Jason. While Quentin was overly concerned with others and suffered over the sins and misfortunes of his family, Jason hasn't a kind word or thought for anyone. A bitter, brutal, and venomous man, he is as contemptuous of his own family as he is of strangers and coworkers, particularly blacks and Jews. Yet he is the only one of the Compson children who has won the love of his mother. Though he despises Benjy, they are alike in that neither of them are capable of showing concern for anyone but themselves. He is disgusted with the promiscuity of his sister and her daughter, yet he keeps a prostitute as a mistress. He remembers even the most trivial slights and holds grudges for years. Jason thinks that he is always right.

This section takes place on Good Friday, the day Christ was crucified, and precedes the **Benjy section** by one day. Two notable aspects of the **Jason section** are the rapid pace of events and the fact that Jason lives almost completely in the present, with little thought for the past or his family's heritage.

Jason, now 35 and the head of the Compson household, tells his mother that Miss Quentin has been skipping school and running around with uncouth people. Mrs. Compson, who was a selfish and ineffectual mother at best and is no better as a grandmother, complains that her "own flesh and blood" has once again disgraced her. Jason asks her if she wants him to discipline Miss Quentin and she reluctantly agrees.

Jason finds Miss Quentin downstairs at breakfast and asks her where she's been spending her time. They argue and Jason takes out his belt to whip her, but Dilsey intervenes. Quentin runs upstairs, passing her grandmother, who has heard the commotion and is on her way downstairs. Angry that his mother has gotten involved, Jason goes outside to the car, waiting to drive Quentin to school. He rebukes Luster for not having changed the tire on the car and demands that he take Benjy around the back of the house so no one can see him.

When Miss Quentin gets in the car, Jason asks her what she did with the money he gave her for school books. She maintains that her mother (Caddy) pays for her books, and Jason replies that Mrs. Compson burns the checks that Caddy sends. Upon hearing this, Quentin tries to tear her dress off and Jason stops the car and threatens to whip her if he hears she's been running around again. Quentin says that she is sorry she was ever born.

Jason is late for work and his boss, Earl, tells him to start assembling the cultivators. He opens a letter from Caddy, who has included a check and asks whether or not Quentin has been receiving the extra money she has been sending. She knows that Jason has been opening her letters to Quentin, and demands that he wire a reply immediately or she will come down to Jefferson.

Jason meets a salesman and they take a break together. They talk about Jews and their supposed control of the stock market. He wires Caddy, then checks on the stock market. He returns to the store and reads a letter from his mistress, Lorraine, who lives in Memphis, then burns the letter. "I make it a rule never to keep a scrap of paper bearing a woman's hand, and I never write them at all," Jason says. He recalls giving her 40 dollars the last time he saw her. Although he claims to believe that money has no value and shouldn't be hoarded, the reader sees numerous examples of his miserliness.

Jason is about to open a third letter, which is addressed to Miss Quentin in Caddy's hand, but he is interrupted several times by customers. He remembers with great bitterness the sale of the pasture to send Quentin to college and Quentin's subsequent suicide, which he views as a betrayal. He thinks about the arrival of Caddy's infant daughter; to him, she is simply another mouth to feed and nearly as big a nuisance as Benjy. He recalls his father's death and his mother forbidding Caddy's name to be spoken in the house.

A fourth letter is from Uncle Maury, who asks to borrow money again. Jason is worried that Caddy will pull another "trick" like she did when Mr. Compson died and she came to the funeral, even though she was not supposed to be in town.

At the time, she offered him one hundred dollars to see her baby for a minute. Jason took the money, got the baby, and held her up in the carriage window as they drove past Caddy. When they came near Caddy, he ordered the driver to speed up. This was his revenge on Caddy for having cost him a job in Herbert Head's bank several years earlier.

Still thinking of when his father died, Jason remembers that Caddy showed up at the store the next day and called him a liar. He told her that she already cost him one job and will now cost him another. He threatened to tell Mrs. Compson and Uncle Maury that she was in town if she did not leave immediately. At first Jason thought his threat would be effective, but suddenly he remembered Dilsey, who would easily let Caddy see her child, and Uncle Maury, who "would do anything for ten dollars."

He ran home to try and scare Dilsey into keeping Caddy away and again thought he had succeeded, until the day that he came home to find Benjy bellowing, a sign that Caddy had been there. He put "the fear of God" into Dilsey and told Caddy that he would fire Dilsey and commit Benjy if she ever tried to visit again. Caddy begged him to be kind to Quentin and promised to send more money if he wanted it. She asked him to let her know if Quentin needed anything, then left.

When Earl goes to lunch, Jason opens Caddy's letter to Quentin and discovers that Caddy has sent a money order for fifty dollars rather than the usual check. He is furious; now he will need Quentin's signature to cash the money order. After his father's death, he had tricked his mother into giving him power of attorney over her, and he is now able to sign her name to any legal document, including checks written to her. Thus he has been confiscating Caddy's checks, giving counterfeit ones to Mrs. Compson to burn, and depositing Caddy's money in Mrs. Compson's account. Mrs. Compson believes that the deposits are Jason's paychecks; meanwhile, he is hoarding his pay for himself. Although Mrs. Compson is completely unaware of Jason's deceitful routine, Quentin and Caddy—and apparently Earl and the town sheriff—have an idea of what he is doing.

As Jason is opening Caddy's letter, Miss Quentin appears and asks whether it is hers. Desperate for the money, she manages to get the letter when Jason leaves the office to wait on a customer, but he returns and slams her hand against the desk drawer until she releases it. He then forces her to sign the money order without allowing her to see the amount and gives her ten dollars, telling her that it is the full amount.

Jason leaves for lunch when Earl returns. After racing around town to find more counterfeit blank checks, he berates the telegraph attendant for not alerting him that his stocks were falling. He goes home for dinner and gives his mother the letter from Caddy with the false check in it, which she burns, and shows her the letter from Uncle Maury. Mrs. Compson complains that she is "depriving" Jason of what is rightfully his by burning Caddy's checks and that she will swallow her pride and accept them if he wants her to. He convinces her to continue burning them and she declares that it is "her place to suffer" for her children. He hears Benjy being fed in the kitchen, and again thinks that he should be sent to Jackson.

Jason stops at the bank to deposit Caddy's check and money order before returning to work. He gets into an argument with Earl, who accuses him of cheating his mother out of a large sum of money. Jason feels glad that he doesn't have a conscience that requires nursing "like a sick puppy all the time," thinks scornfully of his mother's inability to discipline Quentin or any of her own children, and mocks her claim that she comes from a distinguished bloodline.

Around midafternoon, Jason looks up the alley outside the store and sees Quentin with a man in a red tie—the man Benjy sees with Miss Quentin on the porch the following day—sneaking past the shop. He decides to follow them. As he steps into the street, he begins to rail against his family: "one of them is crazy and another one drowned himself and the other one was turned out into the street by her husband"; he thinks that people will believe he is crazy too. He thinks of his father in his final days, who continued to drink even when he became too weak to pour his own drinks. In sharp and revealing contrast to Caddy, Quentin, and his father, Jason claims that the sight of water makes him ill and that he cannot bear to drink alcohol. We later learn that the smell of gasoline gives him blinding headaches and that he uses camphor to cure them, just as his mother does for her many supposed maladies.

Having lost sight of Miss Quentin, he returns to the store to find a telegraph informing him that his account has been closed. He tells Earl that he must run an errand, returns home and takes money from his hidden cache, and passes Quentin and her boyfriend in another car. He follows them out of town into the country but loses sight of them. Finally, he sees their empty car and sets out on foot to find them.

He hears their car engine again and when he returns to his own car, he discovers that they have let the air out of his tire. Cursing his black employees for not replacing the spare tire, he walks five miles into town for a pump. His head is throbbing from the gasoline smell.

He arrives in town after five and discovers another telegram telling him that the value of his stocks has dropped. When he returns to work, Earl expresses concern that the business taking him from work wasn't serious. Here Faulkner seems to link Jason to Quentin and his obsession with time when Jason answers Earl, "You ought to have a dollar watch . . . It won't cost you so much to believe it's lying each time."

At home, Dilsey accuses Jason of following Miss Quentin all afternoon; he denies it. Luster keeps saying that he wants to go to the show, and Jason announces that Earl gave him two free passes. He offers to sell one to Luster for five cents, but Luster has no money. One at a time, he drops the passes into the fire. Dilsey orders him out of the kitchen.

Jason goes to the library. Luster brings in Benjy and stokes the fire so that Benjy can watch it. Benjy rubs his hands on the wall where the mirror used to be. Dilsey calls Jason to supper, but he refuses to come until Mrs. Compson and Quentin come downstairs. At the table, he torments Quentin while his mother asks about his headache. Finally, Quentin begins to cry, declaring that it is Jason who makes her bad. She runs upstairs.

Mrs. Compson asks Jason to be kind to Miss Quentin. She believes that the girl has inherited all the bad traits of Quentin (her son) and Caddy. Mr. Compson, she said, "was always saying that they already knew what cleanliness and honesty were," but look what has become of them. She complains that she and Jason were always treated like outsiders and that the fates of her other children are a judgement on her.

Mrs. Compson goes upstairs and Jason hears her locking Quentin into her room. Later, when he passes Quentin's room and sees the light on, he thinks she is still studying. As he counts the money that he has hidden, he hears Benjy snoring.

The final or **Dilsey section (April Eighth, 1928)** is the only part of the novel in which Faulkner employs a more conventional narrative technique. Although the section focuses on the Compson's black housekeeper, Dilsey, it offers a broader view of its central character than do the other sections of the book. For the first time, the reader sees the Compson family— indeed, Dilsey's family and the town of Jefferson itself—from a broader, more detached perspective.

The **Dilsey section** takes place on Easter Sunday, following the **Benjy section** and Benjy's birthday by one day. (It is significant that most of the novel takes place over Easter weekend, since Faulkner presents Benjy as a sort of impotent Christ figure who is capable of perceiving immorality but unable to take action.) Compared to the inarticulate yearnings of Benjy, the painful, tortured memories of Quentin, and the frenzied pace and rancorous mood of Jason, the **Dilsey section** is measured and peaceful, its main character the only one able to bring order to a chaotic and decaying household.

As the section opens, Dilsey emerges from her cabin dressed for church but wearing old clothes over her good ones. She tests the weather and goes back inside. Faulkner describes the cold, rainy morning, the earth, trees, and birds surrounding the cabin, and Dilsey herself, who has grown gaunt, "as though muscle and tissue had been courage or fortitude which the days or the years had consumed." She reemerges with an umbrella, walks to the woodpile, and begins stacking wood in her arm. She enters the Compson house, dumps the wood into the stove box, dons an apron, and starts a fire. Immediately, she hears Mrs. Compson calling for a hot water bottle and asking whether Dilsey has started breakfast. Dilsey explains that she is late getting started because Luster overslept after going to the show the night before. She sends Mrs. Compson back to bed and calls Luster from the cabin, but he emerges from the cellar of the house. She sends him upstairs to dress Benjy and begins preparing breakfast.

After a few minutes, Mrs. Compson calls downstairs again to ask where Luster is. She wants someone to dress Benjy—even though he isn't awake yet—so that he won't wake Jason on the only day when he can sleep late. She asks where breakfast is and when she can have the hot water bottle. Dilsey finds Luster in the cellar again and sends him up to dress Benjy.

Throughout this section we see Dilsey as a quiet island amid the chaos swirling around her. The moments when she is alone are filled with images of serenity and harmony. After Luster leaves she returns to her work, hearing only "the clock and the fire." She is even able to tell the time from the clock, which has only one hand and is incorrect by three hours.

Luster and Benjy come downstairs. The reader finds the first physical description of Benjy, "a big man who appeared to have been shaped of some substance whose particles would not or did not cohere to one another . . . His hair was pale and fine. . . . His eyes were clear, of the pale sweet blue of cornflowers, his thick mouth hung open, drooling a little." Dilsey sends Luster upstairs to ask Jason if he is ready for breakfast. Luster returns and says that Jason is in a terrible mood because his bedroom window is broken and he thinks that Luster and Benjy are responsible.

Dilsey serves breakfast in the dining room while Luster feeds Benjy. Jason rants about the broken window. Mrs. Compson declares that she never goes into his room where she knows she's "not wanted," and Jason replies that she can't because he's changed the lock and has the only key. Although Miss Quentin sleeps late every Sunday morning, Jason decides that she must join them for breakfast and tells Dilsey to call her. As they hear Dilsey upstairs, Mrs. Compson tells her son that she has given "the darkies" the day off to attend Easter services. He complains that he will have to eat a cold dinner.

Dilsey is still trying to wake Quentin while Jason continues to gripe about the window. When Mrs. Compson observes that it looks as though "somebody had tried to break into the house," Jason suddenly jumps from his chair and runs upstairs. He tries to force open the locked door to Quentin's room, then realizes that his mother has the key. As she comes upstairs, he grabs it from her, calling her an "old fool" and pushing her away. Mrs. Compson begins to wail. Dilsey is afraid that Jason will beat Quentin and stands by.

The room, which has the "dead and stereotyped transience of rooms in assignation houses," is empty. The bed is made. Mrs. Compson tells Dilsey to look for a suicide note, because "Quentin left a note when he did it." She begins rifling through the dresser drawers, but Dilsey stops her and takes her to her room. On the way, they pass Jason's closed door. He is frantically checking his secret cash box, and he discovers that the lock has been broken and the money is gone.

Jason runs downstairs to call the sheriff, ordering him to have a car ready in ten minutes. He storms out of the house without eating his breakfast. Luster wants to know whether Jason has beaten Miss Quentin and Dilsey tells him it isn't his concern and that he should take Benjy outside for a while. Then Luster suggests that Miss Quentin may not have been in her room at all. Dilsey asks him why he would say that, and he explains that he and Benjy saw her climbing out of her window the previous night, as they have seen her do on many other occasions. The two go outside, and Dilsey is alone again. There is no sound.

Dilsey returns to her cabin for a moment, then looks for Benjy and Luster. She finds them in the cellar, where Luster is trying to play music on a sawblade, which he had seen a performer do at the show. With Benjy, Luster, and Luster's mother, Frony, Dilsey heads for church.

Along the way, Frony complains that they shouldn't take Benjy to church with them. Dilsey tells her daughter that the "good Lawd dont keer whether he bright er not" and that those who talk about him are "[t]rash white folks." A group of children dare one another to touch Benjy. Dilsey learns that a minister from St. Louis will preach at the service.

At first, Dilsey does not think much of the visiting preacher, but when he reaches the central idea of his sermon—that they are all cleansed in the blood of the remembered Lamb—she begins weeping. As they leave the church, she remarks that she has "seed de beginnin, en now I sees de endin." Dilsey is referring to the Compson family. She has worked for its members for so long that she feels she was there at its beginning, and now she believes that she is seeing its demise. In truth, Jason, who will never marry, is the last of the Compsons.

Benjy has been quiet since the group left the house for church, but when they reach the Compson house again, he starts moaning. Dilsey straightens Quentin's room and checks on Mrs. Compson, who asks whether a suicide note has been found. Dilsey assures her that Quentin is fine, but Mrs. Compson is more concerned with that fact that Miss Quentin was inconsiderate in not leaving a note. She complains that her son had no reason to kill himself except perhaps to "flout and hurt" her. Dilsey prepares a cold dinner and tells Benjy and Luster to eat because Jason won't be home for lunch.

The narrative then shifts to Jason, who is 20 miles from home. After leaving the Compson place, he drives directly to the sheriff's house, where he demands that they leave at once. The sheriff tells Jason to sit down and explain what happened. Jason tells him that Quentin and her boyfriend have taken the money; the sheriff responds that he doesn't know that for sure. He then asks why Jason had so much money hidden in the house and whether Mrs. Compson knew. Jason angrily replies that it is none of the sheriff's business and again demands that he pursue Quentin at once. When the sheriff asks what he will do if he finds his niece, he says he will do nothing, but raves that she was responsible for his losing a job with Herbert Head, for killing his father and shortening his mother's life, and for sullying his own good name.

In this passage we see a vivid example of Jason's absolute selfishness and his ability to hold grudges and blame anyone but himself for his problems. He is less angry over the missing money than he is over having been "tricked" again—just as he was tricked by Caddy, who was pregnant before she got married (and so cost him a job) and by Quentin who, despite his chance at a good education, committed suicide (thus depriving Jason of a future).

Claiming that he has no proof that Quentin has robbed Jason, the sheriff refuses to pursue her. He accuses Jason of driving the girl away through pure meanness, and suggests that the stolen money does not really belong to him. After issuing a mild threat, Jason leaves. Twice during this scene, the narrator describes the bells ringing in the tower of a nearby black church.

Jason stops at a service station to check his tires and fill his tank, then heads for Mottson, the next stop for the traveling show. He is consumed by thoughts of the bank job that he lost; to him, Miss Quentin and the money have no value except to remind him of what Caddy did to him by becoming pregnant. In his rage, even the world around him seems to be conspiring to keep him from finding his niece: he views the emerging sunshine as "another cunning stroke on the part of the foe," and when he passes an occasional church he curses God, imagining himself and his "file of soldiers . . . dragging Omnipotence down from his throne" if necessary, so that he can get his hands on Quentin.

Jason has developed another violent headache from the gas fumes of the car. He decides not to return home for the camphor that he uses to alleviate the pain. Arriving in Mottson, he asks a man where the show is set up and heads for the grounds, planning to take Quentin and her boyfriend by surprise. Entering one of the two pullman cars there, Jason tries to bully a small, elderly man into telling him where Quentin is, but the man attacks him with a hatchet. Finally, Jason is rescued by other people. "What were you trying to do? commit suicide?" the show manager says.

Sure that he is bleeding from the hatchet blows, Jason is told that he has only hit his head on the rail. He asks about Quentin and her companion and the show manager tells them that he fired them after he learned about the stolen money. By now, Jason's head is throbbing so painfully that he pays a passing black boy to drive him back to Jefferson. Once more, he hears a clock striking the half hour.

At the Compson house, Dilsey sends Benjy and Luster outside and eats her lunch. Alone, she listens for Mrs. Compson but hears nothing. Meanwhile, Luster and Benjy walk near the golf course, causing Benjy to moan when he hears golfers calling their caddies. Luster becomes so annoyed that he whispers Caddy's name several times. Benjy bellows.

Dilsey calls them in and tries without success to comfort Benjy and avoid disturbing Mrs. Compson. Finally, she tells Luster to bring the carriage around and take Benjy for a ride. She warns him to take the exact route that T. P. follows when he takes Benjy out. But Luster spies a group of blacks and decides to show off, so he turns left rather than right at the town monument.

To Benjy, this is utter chaos. He howls more loudly than he ever has, "with scarce interval for breath," his cries filled with "horror; shock; agony eyeless, tongueless." Jason, who is back in town, hears him and rushes to the carriage. He throws Luster aside, takes the reins, and turns the horse around with violent lashes from the whip. Benjy continues to wail and Jason strikes him. He sends Luster back to town and threatens him, "If you ever cross that gate with him again, I'll kill you!"

Luster heads back to the Compson house. As soon as the carriage is turned around, Benjy becomes still. Clutching a broken flower, he serenely watches the shapes of houses flowing past his view, "each in its ordered place."

The Sound and the Fury ends in helpless and inarticulate howling over a disordered world. The Compson family has crumbled into decay. None of its members are capable of forging lasting relationships. In different ways, each of the first three narrators—Benjy, Quentin, and Jason—have become disconnected from moral and physical reality. Traditional values have become meaningless but nothing has replaced them, and the family slides into ruin. Humankind is weak, Faulkner declares, and unless we find a way to rise above our own selfish desires we will perish. Yet in Dilsey, Faulkner also seems to suggest hope: to her, the past is unimportant, the present is vital, and future salvation is our motivation to go on.

Twenty-one years after he wrote *The Sound and the Fury,* Faulkner spoke about man's place in the world. "I decline to accept the end of man," he said. "I believe that man will not merely endure: he will prevail. He is immortal . . . because he has a soul, a spirit capable of compassion and sacrifice and endurance." ✣

—Amy Leal
New York University

Contributing Editor
Therese DeAngelis

List of Characters

Candace or *Caddy Compson*, the only daughter of Jason III and Caroline Compson and the mother of Miss Quentin, is by Faulkner's account the central character of the novel, although she is presented to the reader only through the perceptions of other characters. Her family members have various reactions to her sexual maturation. Benjy, who loves and seeks her, senses her sexual experiences and reacts by howling; Quentin yearns so fiercely to protect her honor that he contemplates admitting to incest with her; Jason abhors her; her mother feels betrayed by her; and her father views her sins with utter detachment, expecting little from females. After brief affairs with Dalton Ames and several other men, she marries Herbert Head on April 25, 1910, when she is two months pregnant with another man's child. They divorce in 1911, and Caddy leaves her child with the Compsons to be raised.

Benjy (formerly *Maury*) *Compson* is the youngest son of Jason Lycurgus Compson III and Caroline Bascomb Compson. At 33 years old, Benjy is an "idiot"; that is, he has the mental capacity of a three-year-old. His parents christen him Maury after his mother's brother, but when his mother realizes his incapacity, she renames him Benjamin. Benjy experiences the world almost exclusively through his senses; he can express himself only by moaning or bellowing. In 1913, after Benjy is thought to have attacked a young girl walking by the Compson house, his brother Jason orders him castrated.

Quentin Compson, the eldest son of Jason and Caroline Compson, desperately wants to preserve Caddy's purity and retain her honor. When it becomes clear that he can do neither, he fantasizes about admitting to, and possibly committing, incest, and about the resulting eternal damnation that would forever link him to his sister. In June 1910, two months after Caddy's wedding, he drowns himself in a river near Cambridge, Massachusetts. On his final day, he is haunted by three memories: Caddy's sexual coming of age and his own impotent efforts to preserve her honor; the sale of Benjy's pasture to pay for his education; and the hopelessness of his fallen family, especially his cold and selfish mother and his cynical, alcoholic father.

Jason Lycurgus Compson IV is the bitter, ambitious, and perversely cruel son of Jason and Caroline Compson. He is a sullen and secretive child; as an adult, he becomes the head of the Compson household and treats his adoring mother with contempt. Quentin's attendance at Harvard still galls him; Benjy's idiocy disgusts him; and Caddy's sexual misbehavior and her divorce—which ruins his chances at a bank job—so enrage him that years later, he blackmails her and steals the money she regularly sends to her daughter. A lifelong bachelor, he maintains a casual and intermittent affair with a woman named Lorraine, who lives in Memphis.

Caroline Bascomb Compson is the wife of Jason Compson III and the mother of Quentin, Caddy, Jason IV, and Benjy. A self-centered, neurotic woman, she insists on the superiority of Bascomb blood over Compson blood and laments that Jason IV is the only one in the family with Bascomb traits. Caddy's fornication is appalling to her not because it is a sin, but because it disgraces her own honor; after Caddy leaves home, she forbids her daughter's name to be spoken. Mrs. Compson spends most of her days in her room feigning illness and sending for Dilsey; she often makes Benjy suffer so that she will not be disturbed.

Jason Lycurgus Compson III is Caroline Compson's husband and the father of Quentin, Caddy, Jason IV, and Benjy. While he seems genuinely fond of his children, he is a weak and ineffectual man, who is unable to offer them more than a dispassionate and nihilistic philosophy of human behavior. In 1912, soon after Caddy's child, Miss Quentin, comes to live with the Compsons, Mr. Compson dies, presumably from alcoholism.

(Miss) Quentin is Caddy's daughter; her father is unknown. Born too soon after Caddy's wedding, she is left to the Compsons to raise. At seventeen, she steals nearly seven thousand dollars from her uncle, Jason IV—money that her mother had been sending to her and that Jason was stealing and keeping for himself—and runs away with a man from a traveling show. No one sees her again.

Dilsey Gibson is the maternal, dignified, and loving black servant who works for the Compsons with her husband, *Roskus.* Her sons, *Versh* and *T. P.*, are Benjy's caretakers when he is young; later in Benjy's life Dilsey's grandson, *Luster*, becomes his keeper. The most moral and humane character in the novel, Dilsey endures with equanimity the whining of Mrs. Compson, the brutality of Jason, the selfishness of Miss Quentin, and the bellowing and howling of Benjy, just as she tolerates the ineptitudes and shortcomings of her own family members. Dilsey brings order and control to the Compson household, just as her section does to Faulkner's novel.

Maury Bascomb is Caroline Compson's alcoholic brother, who sponges off his sister. He pretends to indulge Caroline's hypochondria, but his motivations are selfish; he is either trying to acquire money or gain access to liquor. In early scenes, he sends Caddy and Benjy to deliver messages to Mrs. Patterson, with whom he is having an affair. Later, when his nephew Jason IV is running the Compson household, Maury continues to draw on his sister's funds. ❖

Critical Views

JEAN-PAUL SARTRE ON THE CHRONOLOGY OF *THE SOUND AND THE FURY*

[Jean-Paul Sartre (1905–1980) was a novelist, playwright, and literary critic, as well as the leading exponent of the 20th-century movement in philosophy known as existentialism. Among his critical works are *What Is Literature?* (1949) and studies of Charles Baudelaire (1947), Jean Genet (1952), and Gustave Flaubert (1971–72). In this extract, Sartre explores Faulkner's unusual use of time and chronology to illuminate historical and personal memory in *The Sound and the Fury*.]

In Faulkner, there is never any progression, nothing which can come from the future. The present does not contain in itself the future events we expect—as it seems to when I say that the friend I have been waiting for finally appears. On the contrary, to be present is to appear without reason and to be suspended. Faulkner does not see this suspension in abstract terms; he perceives it in things themselves and tries to make it felt. "The train swung around the curve, the engine puffing with short, heavy blasts, and they passed smoothly from sight that way, with that quality about them of shabby and timeless patience, of static serenity . . ." And again: "Beneath the sag of the buggy the hooves neatly rapid like the motions of a lady doing embroidery, diminishing without progress like a figure on a treadmill being drawn rapidly offstage." Faulkner appears to arrest the motion at the very heart of things; moments erupt and freeze, then fade, recede and diminish, still motionless.

However, this fugitive and incomprehensible state can be grasped and made verbal. Quentin can say: I broke my watch. But when he says it, his gesture will be past. The past can be named and described. Up to a certain point it can be fixed by concepts or intuitively grasped. We have already noted, in connection with *Sartoris*, that Faulkner always shows us events when they are already completed. In *The Sound and the Fury*, everything occurs in the wings; nothing happens, everything has happened. This is what enables us to understand that strange formula of one of the heroes: "I am not is, I was." In this sense also, Faulkner can make of man a being without future, "sum of his climactic experiences," "sum of his misfortunes," "sum of what have you." At every instant we draw a line, since the present is nothing but disordered rumor, a future already past. Faulkner's vision of the world can be compared to that of a man sitting in a convertible looking back. At every moment shadows emerge on his right, and on his left flickering and quavering points of light, which become trees, men, and cars only when they are seen in perspective. The past here gains a surrealistic quality; its outline is hard, clear and immutable. The indefinable and elusive present is helpless before it; it is full of holes through which past things, fixed, motionless and silent, invade it. Faulkner's soliloquies make us think of plane flights made rough by air pockets: at every point the consciousness of the hero "falls into the past" and rises once more, to fall again. The present does not exist, it becomes; everything *was*. In *Sartoris*, the past was seen in terms of "stories" because it consisted of a store of familiar memories and because Faulkner had not yet found his technique. In *The Sound and the Fury* he is more experimental and therefore less certain. But his preoccupation with the past is so strong that he sometimes disguises the present—and the present makes its way in the shadows, like an underground river, to reappear only when it has become past. Thus, Quentin is not even conscious of having insulted Bland, for he is reliving his quarrel with Dalton Ames. And when Bland hits him, the fight is identified with the past fight between Quentin and Ames. Later, Shreve will relate how Bland struck Quentin; he will describe the scene because it has become history—but when it was taking place in the present it was nothing more than a shadowy and obscure event. I have been told of an old school principal whose memory had stopped like a broken watch; it remained forever fixed at his fortieth year. Though he was sixty, he was not aware of his age; his last memory was of the schoolyard and his daily rounds in the playground. Thus he interpreted his present by means of this fixed past and he walked around his table, convinced that he was watching students at their play. Faulkner's characters behave in a similar fashion. Worse than that, their past is not ordered according to chronology but follows certain impulses and emotions. Around some central themes (Caddy's pregnancy, Benjy's castration, Quentin's suicide) innumerable fragments of thought and act revolve. Hence the absurdity of chronology, of "the round and stupid assertion of the clock." The order of the past is the order of the heart. We must not believe that the present event, after it has gone, becomes the most immediate of our memories. The shift of time can submerge it at the bottom of memory or leave it on the surface. Only its own intrinsic value and its relevance to our lives can determine its level.

> —Jean-Paul Sartre, "Time in Faulkner: *The Sound and the Fury* (1939)," *William Faulkner: Two Decades of Criticism*, eds. Frederick J. Hoffman and Olga W. Vickery (East Lansing, MI: Michigan State College Press, 1954), pp. 182–184

❖

JOHN ARTHOS ON THE COMIC ELEMENTS IN *THE SOUND AND THE FURY*

[John Arthos (b. 1908) was a literary critic and a professor of English at the University of Michigan. He is the author of *On the Poetry of Spenser and the Form of the Romantics* (1956), *The Art of Shakespeare* (1964), and *Milton and the Italian Cities* (1968). In the following extract, Arthos examines the conflict between comedy and seriousness in *The Sound and the Fury*.]

It is difficult to preserve humor when the writer considers his work a kind of Passion Week. The strain of inventing rituals and the peculiarly modern difficulties in the way of consecration obscure the perceptions which need to be so finely adjusted in comedy. But to obscure humor is not to kill it, and in much of Faulkner's writing one sees the continuing struggle for comedy. In *The Wild Palms* (where one story is a joke about a convict who returns to jail in order to escape a woman) the humor almost controlled the troubled excitement that elsewhere supports his romanticism. Only in *The Hamlet*, I think, in the characterization of Ratliff and in the incident of the toy cow, do comedy and its lovely reasoning win out.

The curious conflict is apparent in such an elaborately serious work as *The Sound and the Fury*. The story is told in sections presenting the thoughts of four people at certain times over a period of years, when they are thinking mostly about the events of one day, and the effect of that day upon their lives. The central subject of their thought is the seduction of a young girl and its consequences, but the chief interest of the book lies in the description of her brother's attitude toward the catastrophe. He is extremely fond of her, and her situation thrusts upon him a burden of responsibility he accepts as a man who has been brought up in pride of family and delicacy of character. He comes to believe that his own love has failed her, and in something like adolescent self-torment he thinks his guilt is equivalent to the betrayal itself. He extends his torment to the point where it is as if he himself had betrayed her through incest. This straining for guilt places such a burden upon his consciousness that he is unequal to it, and finally he kills himself.

The problem appears ridiculous (the comic writer turning in his sleep), but it is not intrinsically so. If the brother's concern is justified, as it certainly is, we are tempted to mock him because he is only flirting with despair. As his father tells him (they have been talking of death): "you seem to regard it merely as an experience that will whiten your hair overnight so to speak without altering your appearance at all." The brother tries to understand what sin is, but he cannot; and yet he thinks he must assume his sister's guilt. His confusion drives him mad. He wants to believe in original sin, he wants to make himself into a symbol of it, and he finds himself unable to through some defect of insight and understanding. Accordingly, the plot of the novel is resolved through an explicit demonstration of meaninglessness of an historic doctrine. A generous man, dedicated to something without meaning, finds his end in absurdity and madness. The absurdity is obvious, but not obvious enough to be presented comically. The author's sympathy prevents the detachment necessary for comedy, and even the meaning of the calamity is blurred. No meaningful comment is offered to present a larger view than Quentin Compson's own, no more than is found in a poem called "Visions in Spring," where the author speaks of himself as one

> who toiled through corridors of harsh laughter,
> Who sought for light in dark reserves of pain. . . .

On the other hand, the idiot brother, Benjy, the most vivid character in the book, achieves symbolic significance. His mind is like a shattered mirror, and he understands very little of what goes on about him. But the fragments of his mind reflect everything, not merely a single evil, and everything that he sees is transformed, as it were, purely and without distortion, into a continuous moan. Benjy is the embodiment of disintegration, the mind shattered by the pain of evil, and Faulkner implies that the sound he makes is the music of the spheres. As such its disharmony is the mingling of the cries rising into the minds of all the characters in the story and in the world. Evil is thus represented as the world's invasion of the individual soul, where once it was merely a bullet, fired at some time in the past, and still wounding a lieutenant.

> —John Arthos, "Ritual and Humor in the Writing of William Faulkner (1948)," *William Faulkner: Two Decades of Criticism*, eds. Frederick J. Hoffman and Olga W. Vickery (East Lansing, MI: Michigan State College Press, 1954), pp. 107–108

❦

RALPH ELLISON ON FAULKNER'S DEPICTION OF THE "SOUTHERN NEGRO"

[Ralph Ellison (1914–1994) was an American novelist, critic, and essayist. His best-known work of fiction was his first novel, *The Invisible Man* (1952). In addition to his introduction to Stephen Crane's *The Red Badge of Courage* and *Four Great Stories* (1960), he also wrote two collections of essays, *Shadow and Act* (1953) and *Going to the Territory* (1986). In the following extract, taken from his earlier essay collection, Ellison examines Faulkner's protrayal of blacks as symbolic of both rebellion and repression.]

⟨. . .⟩ it is the creative function of myth to protect the individual from the irrational, and since it is here in the realm of the irrational that, impervious to science, the stereotype grows, we see that the Negro stereotype is really an image of the unorganized, irrational forces of American life, forces through which, by projecting them in forms of images of an easily dominated minority, the white individual seeks to be at home in the vast unknown world of America. Perhaps the object of the stereotype is not so much to crush the Negro as to console the white man.

Certainly there is justification for this view when we consider the work of William Faulkner. In Faulkner most of the relationships which we have pointed out between the Negro and contemporary writing come to focus: the social and the personal, the moral and the technical, the nineteenth-century emphasis upon morality and the modern accent upon the personal myth. And on the strictly literary level he is prolific and complex enough to speak for those Southern writers who are aggressively anti-negro and for those younger writers who appear most sincerely interested in depicting the Negro as a rounded human being. What is more, he is the greatest artist the South has produced. While too complex to be given more than a glance in these notes, even a glance is more revealing of what lies back of the distortion of the Negro in modern writing than any attempt at a group survey might be.

Faulkner's attitude is mixed. Taking his cue from the Southern mentality in which the Negro is often dissociated into a malignant stereotype (the bad nigger) on the one hand and a benign stereotype (the good nigger) on the other, most often Faulkner presents characters embodying both. The dual function of the dissociation seems to be that of avoiding moral pain and thus to justify the South's racial code. But since such a social order harms whites no less than blacks, the sensitive Southerner, the artist, is apt to feel its effects acutely—and within the deepest levels of his personality. For not only is the social division forced upon the Negro by the ritualized ethic of discrimination, but upon the white man by the strictly enforced set of anti-Negro taboos. The conflict is always with him. Indeed, so rigidly has the recognition of Negro humanity been tabooed that the white Southerner is apt to associate any form of personal rebellion with the Negro. So that for the Southern artist the Negro becomes a symbol of his personal rebellion, his guilt and his repression of it. The Negro is thus a compelling object of fascination, and this we see very clearly in Faulkner.

—Ralph Ellison, *Shadow and Act* (New York: Random House, 1953), pp. 41–42

❖

OLGA W. VICKERY ON THE THEMATIC AND PLOT STRUCTURE OF *THE SOUND AND THE FURY*

[Olga W. Vickery (1925–1970) was a Faulkner scholar who taught at a number of universities and colleges, including Lake Forest College, Purdue University, and the University of California at Riverside. She is the author of *The Novels of William Faulkner* (1959), and coedited *William Faulkner: Three Decades of Criticism* (1960). In this extract, Vickery explores structure in *The Sound and the Fury*.]

The Sound and the Fury was the first of Faulkner's novels to make the question of form and technique an unavoidable critical issue. In any discussion of its structure the controlling assumption should be that there are plausible reasons for the particular arrangement of the four sections and for the use of the stream of consciousness technique in the first three and not in the fourth. Jean-Paul Sartre's comment that the moment the reader attempts to isolate the plot content "he notices that he is telling another story" indicates the need for such an assumption, not only for any light that may be thrown on *The Sound and the Fury* but for any insight that may emerge concerning Faulkner's method and achievement.

The structure of the novel is clearly reflected in the organization of the events of the evening on which Damuddy dies. These events reveal the typical gestures and reactions of the four children to each other and to the mysterious advent of death. They chart the range and kind of each to their responses to a new experience. In this way the evening partakes of the dual nature of the novel: primarily it is an objective, dramatic scene revealing the relations and tensions which exist among the children, but at the same time it is a study in perspective. Between the fact of Damuddy's death and the reader stands not only the primitive mind of the narrator, Benjy, but the diverse attitudes of the other children and the deliberate uncommunicativeness of the adults.

Within the novel as a whole it is Caddy's surrender to Dalton Ames which serves both as the source of dramatic tension and as the focal point for the various perspectives. This is evident in the fact that the sequence of events is not caused by her act—which could be responded to in very different ways—but by the significance which each of her brothers actually attributes to it. As a result, the four sections appear quite unrelated even though they repeat certain incidents and are concerned with the same problem, namely Caddy and her loss of virginity. Although there is a progressive revelation or rather clarification of the plot, each of the sections is itself static. The consciousness of each character becomes the actual agent illuminating and being illuminated by the central situation. Everything is immobilized in this pattern; there is no development of either character or plot in the traditional manner. This impression is reinforced not only by the shortness of time directly involved in each section but by the absence of any shifts in style of the kind that, for example, accompany the growing maturity of Cash Bundren in *As I Lay Dying*.

By fixing the structure while leaving the central situation ambiguous, Faulkner forces the reader to reconstruct the story and to apprehend its significance for himself. Consequently, the reader recovers the story at the same time as he grasps the relation of Benjy, Quentin, and Jason to it. This, in turn, is dependent on his comprehension of the relation between the present and the past events with which each of the first three sections deals. As he proceeds from one section to the next, there is a gradual clarification of events, a rounding out of the fragments of scenes and conversations which Benjy reports. Thus, with respect to the plot the four sections are inextricably connected, but with respect to the central situation they are quite distinct and self-sufficient. As related to the central focus, each of the first three sections presents a version of the same facts which is at once the truth and a complete distortion of the truth. It would appear, then, that the theme of *The Sound and the Fury,* as revealed by the structure, is the relation between the act and man's apprehension of the act, between the event and the interpretation. The relation is by no means a rigid or inelastic thing but is a matter of shifting perspective, for, in a sense, each man creates his own truth. This does not mean that the truth does not exist or that it is fragmentary or that it is unknowable; it only insists that truth is a matter of the heart's response as well as the mind's logic.

—Olga W. Vickery, *The Novels of William Faulkner* (Baton Rouge, LA: Louisiana State University Press, 1959), pp. 28–29

❖

FREDERICK J. HOFFMAN ON CADDY'S AFFAIR WITH DALTON AMES

[Frederick J. Hoffman (1909–1967) taught at the University of California at Riverside, where he specialized in American literature. Among his publications are *Freudianism and the Literary Mind* (1945), *The Modern Novel in America* (1951), and *The Growth of American Literature*, 2 vols. (1956). In the following extract, taken from William Faulkner (1961), Hoffman explores the significance of Caddy's affair with Dalton Ames and comments on Faulkner's narrative strategy.]

The central event of *The Sound and the Fury* is Candace's (Caddy's) affair with Dalton Ames. It is her "sin," her breach of ethics or contract, her act of bringing the outside world within the Compson family pattern. It is seen "out of proportion" in each of the first three sections; it is re-examined in part four and there seen as far less important than it had been earlier. Faulkner gives both an inner and an outer view of it. He moves from one kind of subjective view to another, finally into the world itself, so that we may gaze at the place and the site of its happening. Truth would seem, therefore, to be a matter of perspective; we are aware not so much of truth itself but of a version of the truth, a distortion of it, which must be set right, and eventually is. Above all, Faulkner is saying that any truth is far more complex than it appears on the surface to be.

As we already know, Faulkner spoke in his interview with Mrs. Stein of "the picture. . . . of the muddy seat of a little girl's drawers . . ." (*Three Decades*, 73). The incident occurs in 1898; Caddy, playing with her brothers in the "branch," tries to rub out the stain, but does not succeed: "Just look at you," she says, "It done soaked clean through onto you." (*SF*, 93) The stain becomes the sin of her affairs, leading to Miss Quentin, the illegitimate child; and in the end the image of the mud stain is replaced "by the one of the fatherless and motherless girl climbing down the rainpipe to escape from the only home she had, where she had never been offered love or affection or understanding" (*Three Decades*, 73). The first three sections of the novel are concerned with the three distinct views of Caddy's "stain." Caddy means something different in each case; Mrs. Vickery has described it in *Novels* (30): "For Benjy she is the smell of the trees; for Quentin, honor; and for Jason, money or at least the means of obtaining it." In part four, Caddy all but disappears, though her role in Jason's conflict with Miss Quentin is quite clearly in the background.

Faulkner adjusts the style, the imagery, and the narrative sequence of each of the sections to the point of view from which it is being written. Benjy's world is a fixed one, a world of sensations, one without time: all of these characteristics come from the fact that he is a thirty-three-year-old idiot who stopped growing mentally in 1898 at the age of three. He cannot abstract or generalize, cannot distinguish between one time and another, and can only react to a number of fixed sensory conditions that repeat themselves to him again and again. Here memory and sense are inseparable: a thirty-year difference in time is no difference at all, and sensations that are actually separated by twenty or thirty years are undifferentiated.

—Frederick J. Hoffman, *William Faulkner* (New York: Twayne Publishers, 1961), pp. 51–53

❖

PETER SWIGGART ON JASON'S MONOLOGUE IN *THE SOUND AND THE FURY*

[Peter Swiggart is an author and Faulkner scholar. In the following extract, taken from *The Art of Faulkner's Novels* (1962), he examines in detail the third section and the character of Jason in *The Sound and the Fury*.]

The third monologue in *The Sound and the Fury* is that of Quentin's younger brother, Jason, whose absolute corruption is a grotesque reflection of Quentin's more complex failure. Jason appears in the first two sections only as a spoiled crybaby and tattletale, with a penchant for petty shopkeeping and secret maneuvering. His fate, like that of his brother's, is linked to Caddy's downfall. Jason is outraged by her actions, but the reason for his hatred is the perverse conviction that her behavior has cost him the banking job promised by Herbert Head, Caddy's fiancé. This sense of injury is Jason's justification for stealing the money which Caddy sends to Jefferson for the support of her daughter.

The organization of Jason's sections is based upon his two primary obsessions, his quest for the "golden fleece" of financial profit and his hatred of both Caddy and her daughter Quentin. Much of his monologue narration is devoted to business affairs, in particular his exploitation of the two women and his futile efforts to make money by cotton speculation. Other sections of his narration are devoted to a flashback account of Mr. Compson's funeral, where Jason's financial arrangements with Caddy are initially made, and to his disastrous efforts to catch his niece with her carnival lover, "a man that would wear a red tie" (260).

It is significant that "time" for Jason is the equivalent of money. His practical obsession with the passage of time is a virtual parody of Quentin's more philosophical concern. Perrin Lowrey has shown in detail how Jason can never catch up with the fast-moving events around him. He dashes convulsively from place to place, always trying to get somewhere and always being late. His cotton speculation is a case in point. The market is so unpredictable that Jason has to keep on the alert for any sudden rise or fall. Time gets the better of him when an important message comes through while he is out spying on his niece. He arrives at the telegraph office an hour after the cotton market has closed. Jason's method of exploiting Caddy is to accept and cash her checks in his mother's name. Mrs. Compson mistakenly thinks that the checks she is burning represent Caddy's tainted income, and that the money regularly paid into her account comes from Jason's salary. However, Jason has run out of blank checks to prepare for his mother's ritual of destruction and must search frantically, with very little time, for check blanks that will do.

Jason's hatred of Caddy is related to his most characteristic phobia, the smell of gasoline. Mrs. Compson says that Jason has had this weakness since a child, but it might well have originated with the car which Caddy's fiancé gives her, and which reminds Jason of his lost job. Jason's own car is paid for with the money originally used to buy him a share in the general merchandise store where he works. The headaches from the gasoline fumes cause Jason great trouble, in the final section of the novel, when he tries to recover the money stolen by his niece.

He has no camphor-soaked handkerchief to allay the gas smell, and the drugstores are all closed on Sunday. His headaches and the use of camphor relate him to his mother, who uses her illness as a focal-point for self-pity and often as a means to escape or reject her responsibilities. Like his brother

Quentin, Jason never drinks alcohol—a frequent sign in Faulkner's work of moral impotency. Even Benjy gets drunk on "sasprilluh." The virginal Quentin neither smokes nor drinks, but during his last day he buys his first cigar and takes two puffs before giving it away. Like the cigarette rolled by Dalton Ames and the expensive cigars which Herbert Head imports from Havana, this cigar which Quentin cannot smoke seems intended as a sign of masculinity.

In spite of his ruthless treatment of others, Jason's mind is filled with moral clichés traceable to the family tradition of public integrity and personal honor. Like Quentin, who cleans his vest and brushes his teeth before committing suicide, Jason has a ludicrous concern for personal appearance. His selfishness and cruelty are known to everyone, yet he refers constantly to his mother's "good name" and the family's "position" in the community. Jason even convinces himself that he is the loyal guardian of his niece Quentin. Seeing her play truant from school with a boy friend from the circus, he gives reckless chase: "Me, without any hat, in the middle of the afternoon, having to chase up and down back alleys because of my mother's good name. Like I say you cant do anything with a woman like that, if she's got it in her. If it's in her blood, you cant do anything with her. The only thing you can do is to get rid of her, let her go on and live with her own sort" (250). Outwitted by the pair, Jason shifts his self-dramatization to that of a betrayed uncle: "It's not playing a joke that any eight year old boy could have thought of, it's letting your own uncle be laughed at by a man that would wear a red tie" (260). Jason is a product of a decayed gentility and not, like Flem Snopes of *The Hamlet*, a symbolic outsider devoid of any feeling for morality and justice. His cruelty rests to a great extent upon self-deception and is heightened dramatically by his role as a genuine though perverted Compson.

—Peter Swiggart, *The Art of Faulkner's Novels* (Austin, TX: University of Texas Press, 1962), pp. 101–103

❖

JOHN W. HUNT ON QUENTIN'S MORAL OUTLOOK

[John W. Hunt (b. 1927) is the Dean of the Center of Arts and Sciences at Lehigh University and the author of many journal articles. He edited *Adversity and Grace in Recent American Fiction* (1968) and wrote *William Faulkner: Art in Theological Tension* (1965), from which this extract is taken. Hunt explores Quentin's "myopic moralism" regarding Caddy's sexuality.]

The tradition testifies that Quentin is rationally right in focusing upon Caddy's frail chastity. His rationalistic and moralistic sensibility allows him to salvage from the tradition only an ability to identify its talismans, its fetishes, and does not afford him a vision beyond the *mise en scéne* to the vital spirit generating the code itself. In his mind, his inherited concept of honor (and thus the status of meaning) is more than figuratively supported "by the minute fragile membrane of her maidenhead" (SF, 9). It is also true that the decline and fall of the Compson family is paced by the decline and fall of the woman from a position of virtuous eminence. Not only in Caddy but also in his mother does Quentin find no assent to the moral vision of which the code was a rationalization. Brooks is therefore right when he says that the failure of Quentin's mother is just as crucial as Caddy's failure and has a great deal to do with Caddy's incapacity. Herbert Head's bourgeois excuse for his past ("I never had a mother like yours to teach me the finer points") heightens the poignancy of Quentin's inner cry, "*My little sister had no. If I could say Mother. Mother,*" and again, "*if I'd just had a mother so I could say Mother Mother.*" Quentin has no mother; he does not enjoy the matriarchal structure under which the code of honor functions to provide meaning.

Quentin's obsession with sex—and it is that—certainly goes beyond its function in his inherited code. He is sick with his sister's honeysuckle sweet sex, but he is also perversely attracted to it. When Caddy finds him in the barn during the rain with Natalie "*dancing sitting down,*" he jumps into the hog wallow, in a highly symbolic action, and smears her with mud. Benjy, of course, is sensitive to Caddy's loss of chastity too, and also relates to her sexually, but his attraction is, in the novel's dramatic context, less perverted, more innocent, less moralistic, more moral and forgiving.

Caddy's failure is not from sheer perversity; she fails in Quentin's terms, not her own. Her experiments in sex are "natural," if foolish. She is capable of compassion and love, as her relationship with Benjy and her love for Dalton Ames illustrate. The pathetic irony of Quentin's situation comes from his incapacity, not hers. She is capable—or was before he corrupted her—of the natural power and fertility of the matriarch. Caddy actually functions as a mother to Benjy. When, during Quentin's second phase, she succumbs to his rationalistic moralism, she divests herself of that sovereignty essential to the matriarch—the sovereignty above the rules. Quentin's agony, arising from his myopic moralism, is heightened by the fact that he has not only a promiscuous sister, but also a sister who will not admit, does not know, and cannot believe that her promiscuity involves anything more than a private and personal doom.

—John W. Hunt, *William Faulkner: Art in Theological Tension* (Syracuse, NY: Syracuse University Press, 1965), pp. 56–57

❖

CLEANTH BROOKS ON THE FOUR POINTS OF VIEW PRESENTED IN *THE SOUND AND THE FURY*

[Cleanth Brooks (1906–1994) was an influential critic, editor, and author, as well as the managing editor of the *Southern Review* with Robert Penn Warren. Brooks wrote *Modern Poetry and Tradition* (1935) and *William Faulkner: First Encounters* (1983). In the following extract, taken from *William Faulkner* (1966), Brooks examines Faulkner's use of varying points of view to tell the history of the Compson family.]

The salient technical feature of *The Sound and the Fury* is the use of four different points of view in the presentation of the breakup of the Compson family. This special technique was obviously of great personal consequence to Faulkner, as evidenced by his several references to it in the last few years. The story is told through one obsessed consciousness after another, as we pass from Benjy's near-mindlessness to the obsessed mind of Quentin and then to the very differently obsessed mind of Jason. The first three sections are all examples of the stream-of-consciousness method, and yet, as Lawrence Bowling has well observed, how different they are in movement, mood, and effect!

The reader's movement through the book is a progression from murkiness to increasing enlightenment, and this is natural, since we start with the mind of an idiot, go on next through the memories and reveries of the Hamlet-like Quentin, and come finally to the observations of the brittle, would-be rationalist Jason. Part of the sense of enlightenment comes simply from the fact that we are traversing the same territory in circling movements, and the cumulative effect of names and characterizations begins to dramatize for us with compelling urgency a situation we have come to accept almost as our own.

Readers of this novel some thirty years ago were shocked at what seemed an almost willful obscurity, and the difficulties entailed by Faulkner's method are not to be minimized. Some passages in Quentin's section, for example, seem to me so private as to be almost incomprehensible. But a generation of sensitive readers has testified to the almost palpable atmosphere of the first sections of the book. We do learn what it is like to live in such a family through being forced to share the minds of the three brothers in their special kinds of obsession. The sense of frustration and "entrapment" is overpowering. Benjy is obviously a victim in the sense in which an animal is, but Quentin is hardly less so, and even the horribly "sane" Jason feels victimized, as he shows in his compulsive talk. There is, therefore, as we move toward the end of the book, the sense of coming out into an objective world, a world in which objects take on firmness of outline and density and weight, in which objective truth, and not mere obsessional impressions, exists. Though the fourth section is not passed through Dilsey's mind, it is dominated by Dilsey; and the world in which Dilsey moves is an objective world, not simply the projection of a distempered spirit.

—Cleanth Brooks, *William Faulkner* (New Haven: Yale University Press, 1966), pp. 325–26

❖

JOSEPH BROGUNIER ON THE INFLUENCE OF A. E. HOUSMAN ON *THE SOUND AND THE FURY*

[Joseph Brogunier teaches at the University of Maine and was editor of the journal *Modern Fiction Studies,* from which the following extract was taken. Brogunier explores the influence of the English poet A. E. Housman, one of Faulkner's favorite authors, on *The Sound and the Fury*.]

In numerous interviews Faulkner listed his favorite authors, writers to whom he returned again and again; and they were often those he had first read as a young man. At the end of one such list, in the Paris Review interview of 1956, Faulkner mentioned that he "still read Housman," implying that at one time he had read him a great deal more. ⟨. . .⟩ as a young man he not only was outspokenly enthusiastic about Housman but also was influenced by him in several works.

⟨. . .⟩ Housman's imprint appears in the tone and substance of some of Faulkner's novels; on *The Sound and the Fury* especially he has had an heretofore unrecognized and sizable influence.

Housman's influence on the novels dates, in fact, from Faulkner's first—*Soldiers' Pay*. When the wounded Donald Mahon's effects are sent to his father, the rector, among them is an apparent duplicate of the paperbound copy of *A Shropshire Lad* Faulkner had found in a bookshop, a mute commentary upon the harshness, destructiveness, and malignity of the world into which the young man was born and of the war in which he fought. And his father, the rector, who while standing against the blows of this world shows himself to be a strongly stoic character, may be so in part because of the stoicism Faulkner found in Housman. In *The Sound and the Fury*, Robert Penn Warren has pointed out that Mr. Compson's stoic advice to his son—that "we must just stay awake and see evil done for a little while"—is a paraphrase of Housman's line "Let us endure an hour and see injustice done." In addition, it should be noted that Mr. Compson's paraphrase implies an irony apparently unrecognized by him, for he intends it as consolatory advice to a son who is contemplating suicide, and yet it derives from a poem that pictures man's life as full of barely supportable pain and sorrow, that praises the incorporeal, prebirth state of his soul as a refuge from these ills, and that concludes by asking, "when shall I sleep again?" Thirteen years later Faulkner seems to have adapted Housman's line again, using it this time less ironically, however, and as more fully emblematic of the quality of endurance. In the debate in the commissary between Ike and McCaslin in *Go Down, Moses*, the young Ike speaks of the economic oppression of the Negroes, characterizing it as "Binding them for a while yet, a little while yet." The speech is a close echo of Mr. Compson's advice and seems to be, in substance and tone, another paraphrase of Housman's line. Both Ike's speech and Housman's line refer to the duration of evil and the enduring of evil (immediately following in the passage Faulkner in fact uses Housman's word "endure"—"they will endure"), and both have a tone of mixed resignation and hope. In addition, though Ike clearly believes the Negroes will win release from their oppression in the generations to come, an ironic implication resides in the fact that their other release, and the only one that many will have, is that same death Housman's poem advances as the relief of all ills.

—Joseph Brogunier, "The Housman Source in *The Sound and the Fury*," *Modern Fiction Studies* 18, No. 2 (Summer 1972): 220, 221–222

❖

GEORGE C. BEDELL ON JEAN-PAUL SARTRE'S CRITIQUE OF *THE SOUND AND THE FURY*

[George C. Bedell (b. 1928), a literary critic and author, is the Director of Humanities and Fine Arts at the State University System of Florida at Tallahassee. He coauthored *Introduction to Religion in America* (1975). In the following extract, taken from *Kierkegaard and Faulkner: Modalities of Existence* (1972), Bedwell refutes Jean-Paul Sartre's argument that "nothing happens" in *The Sound and the Fury,* arguing that Sartre fails to distinguish between Faulkner and his characters.]

Jean-Paul Sartre's now celebrated article on Faulkner examines time in *The Sound and the Fury* by first calling attention to the way in which this novelistic *tour de force* is constructed: "Faulkner did not think in terms of an orderly narrative and then shuffle the parts like a pack of cards." To think of it in this way is to miss the point entirely. Rather, the order of the novel reflects a way of perceiving the world. Faulkner told the Compson story as he saw and understood it and "could not have told the story in any other way." He, of course, was seeking new fictional strategies and was following the lead of writers like Joseph Conrad and Ford Madox Ford who had experimented with the idea of writing novels with a deliberately confused and dislocated time sequence. Many were at first "put off" by the narrative sequence in *The Sound and the Fury.* Recognition of the effectiveness of Faulkner's style came only after Conrad Aiken spoke up in 1939:

> If one considers these queer sentences not simply by themselves, as monsters of grammar or awkwardness, but in their relation to the book as a whole, one sees a functional reason and necessity for their being as they are. They parallel in a curious and perhaps inevitable way, and not without aesthetic justification, the whole elaborate method of *deliberately withheld meaning,* of progressive and partial and delayed disclosure, which so often gives characteristic shape to the novels themselves. It is a persistent offering of obstacles, a calculated system of screens and obtrusions, of confusions and ambiguous interpolations and delays, with one express purpose; and that purpose is simply to keep the form—and the idea—fluid and

unfinished, still in motion, as it were, and unknown, until the dropping into place of the very last syllable.

But Sartre's contention is that, with all its technical virtuosity, "nothing happens" in *The Sound and the Fury*; "the story does not progress." He attributes this suspension of forward action to what he calls Faulkner's "metaphysic of time," which he claims ends up destroying time. In addition to Faulkner he mentions Proust, Joyce, Dos Passos, Gide, and Virginia Woolf. He says that some of them have deprived time "of past and future and reduced it to the pure intuition of the moment; others, like Dos Passos, make it a limited and mechanical memory. Proust and Faulkner have simply decapitated it; they have taken away its future—that is to say, the dimension of free choice and act." Sartre's criticism, then, has little to do with Faulkner's methods. What he does review is the metaphysic which informs *The Sound and the Fury*.

If we examine Sartre's essay carefully, however, we soon discover, as many recent critics have, that Sartre makes no distinction between Faulkner and his characters. As John W. Hunt puts it, "one need not deny that psychologically driven, haunted, and confused people populate [Faulkner's] novels, but it is a mistake to conclude that because his characters are confused he himself is confused." There is no doubt that violence, chaos, and decadence are themes which resonate throughout the Faulkner canon, but they are part of his grand strategy. And we must not conclude that they are there "because Faulkner himself is at home in this murkey, demonic world,' or because his 'psyche is completely out of control.'" Instead, they are 'part of a total vision which gathers all kinds of attitudes toward time under the umbrella of his own understanding of the nature of time.

Sartre, however, does not see this. He takes hold of one particular attitude toward time that is displayed by a type of character that appears in the novels and calls that attitude Faulkner's.

⟨. . .⟩ It may well be that "it is man's misfortune to be confined in time," but it does not necessarily follow that "this is the true subject of the novel." It is clearly one of the major motifs, but in the last or Dilsey section of the novel, there is yet another motif which contradicts the idea that man is enthralled in time. In this section we are led to believe that man is able to transcend time and to endure "the slings and arrows of outrageous fortune." Dilsey's language, her whole way of being in the world, is manifestly transcendent. For her, it is not a misfortune *to be* in time, because man's destiny (*her* destiny) is caught up in the "ricklickshun en de blood of de Lamb!" This must be considered of the essential Faulkner as much as the Quentin section, because one cannot arbitrarily choose one motif over another and identify it with the author.

—George C. Bedell, *Kierkegaard and Faulkner: Modalities of Existence* (Baton Rouge, LA: Louisiana State University Press, 1972), pp. 184–186, 187

❖

JOHN T. IRWIN ON QUENTIN'S SUICIDE AND HIS DUAL NATURE

[John T. Irwin (b. 1940) is a poet and critic who has taught at Johns Hopkins University and has served as editor of the *Georgia Review*. In the following extract, taken from *Doubling and Incest/Repetition and Revenge: A Speculative Reading of Faulkner* (1975), Irwin explores the dual nature of Quentin's psychology as revealed in both *The Sound and the Fury* and *Absalom, Absalom!,* and Quentin's drowning himself with his attempts to escape his own shadow on the day of his suicide.]

Both the narcissistic origin of doubling and the scenario of madness leading to the suicidal murder of the double help to illuminate the internal narrative of Quentin Compson's last day given in *The Sound and the Fury* and in turn to illuminate the story he tells in *Absalom*. In the fictive time of the novels, Quentin and Shreve's joint narration, which occupies the last half of *Absalom,* takes place in January 1910, and Quentin's suicide occurs six months later on June 2, 1910, but the account of that suicide is given in a novel that appeared seven years before *Absalom*. Since we already know Quentin's end when we observe his attempt in *Absalom* to explain the reason for Bon's murder, we not only participate in that effort but also engage at the same time in an analogous effort of our own to explain Quentin's murder of himself. And it is only when we see in the murder of Bon by Henry what Quentin saw in it—that Quentin's own situation appears to be a repetition of the earlier story—that we begin to understand the reason for Quentin's suicide. And this whole repetitive structure is made even more problematic by the fact that the explanation which Quentin gives for Bon's murder (that Bon is black, i.e., the shadow self) may well be simply the return of the repressed—simply an unconscious projection of Quentin's own psychic history. Quentin's situation becomes endlessly repetitive insofar as he constantly creates the predecessors of that situation in his narration of past events. And to escape from that kind of repetition, one must escape from the self.

Like Narcissus, Quentin drowns himself, and the internal narrative of his last day, clearly the narrative of someone who has gone insane, is dominated by Quentin's obsessive attempts to escape from his shadow, to "trick his shadow," as he says. When Quentin leaves his dormitory on the morning of his death, the pursuit begins: "The shadow hadn't quite cleared the stoop. I stopped inside the door, watching the shadow move. It moved almost perceptibly, creeping back inside the door, driving the shadow back into the door . . . The shadow on the stoop was gone. I stepped into the sunlight, finding my shadow again. I walked down the steps just ahead of it." Later, standing by the river, he looks down:

> "The shadow of the bridge, the tiers of the railing, my shadow leaning flat upon the water, so easily had I tricked it that it would not quit me. At least fifty feet it was, and if I only had something to blot it into the water, holding it until it was drowned, the shadow of the package like two shoes wrapped up lying on the water. Niggers say a drowned man's shadow was watching him in the water all the time" (p. 109).

Like Narcissus staring at his image in the pool, Quentin stares at his shadow in the river and, significantly, makes a reference to Negroes in relation to that shadow. I say "significantly" because at crucial points during Quentin's last day this connection between the shadow and the Negro recurs, most notably on the tram ride down to the river when Quentin sits next to a black man:

> "I used to think that a Southerner had to be always conscious of niggers. I thought that Northerners would expect him to. When I first came East I kept thinking You've got to remember to think of them as colored people not niggers, and if it hadn't happened that I wasn't thrown with many of them, I'd have wasted a lot of time and trouble before I learned that the best way to take all people, white or black, is to take them for what they think they are, then leave them alone. That was when I realised that a nigger is not a person so much as a form of behavior; a sort of obverse reflection of the white people he lives among" (p. 105).

If, in Quentin's mind, blacks are the "obverse reflection" of whites, if they are like shadows, then in Quentin's narrative projection of his own psychodrama in *Absalom*, Charles Bon's role as the dark seducer, as the shadow self, is inevitably linked with Bon's Negro blood. Further, since Quentin's own shadow has Negro resonances in his mind, it is not surprising that on the day of his suicide Quentin, who is being pursued by his shadow, is told by one of the three boys that he meets walking in the country that he (Quentin) talks like a colored man, nor is it surprising that another of the boys immediately asks the first one if he isn't afraid that Quentin will hit him.

If Quentin's determination to drown his shadow represents the substitutive punishment, upon his own person, of the brother seducer (the dark self, the ego shadowed by the unconscious) by the brother avenger (the bright self, the ego controlled by the superego), then it is only appropriate that the events from Quentin's past that obsessively recur during the internal narrative leading up to his drowning are events that emphasize Quentin's failure as both brother avenger and brother seducer in relation to his sister Candace—failures which his drowning of himself is meant to redeem.

> —John T. Irwin, *Doubling and Incest/Repetition and Revenge: A Speculative Reading of Faulkner* (Baltimore: Johns Hopkins University Press, 1975), pp. 35–37

❖

ANDRÉ BLEIKASTEN ON *THE SOUND AND THE FURY* AND LITERARY MODERNISM

[André Bleikasten is a French scholar who has translated Faulkner's *As I Lay Dying* into French. He has
written numerous journal articles on Faulkner, as well
as a critical volume, *The Ink of Melancholy: Faulkner's
Novels from* The Sound and the Fury *to* Light in August
(1990). In the following extract, from *The Most
Splendid Failure: Faulkner's* The Sound and the Fury
(1976), Bleikasten places the novel in the context of
other works of literary modernism as part of the
"great tradition of failure."]

It is interesting to note that like many great modern novels—
Ulysses and *The Magic Mountain* come at once to mind—*The
Sound and the Fury* began by taking the form of a short story in
the mind of its creator. The novel form was resorted to as a *pis
aller* <last resource>, and the book may thus be seen as the
outgrowth of an initial failure: Faulkner's incapacity to complete the narrative within the limits of the short story, which
he considered "the most demanding form after poetry." What
is more, failure informs the very pattern of the novel, since
the four sections it consists of represent as many vain
attempts at getting the story told. Most readers will of course
protest that the sum of these failures is a success, and dismiss
this confession of impotence as an excess of modesty. Yet
Faulkner's insistence on his failure was no pose. Experience
had already taught him that "being a writer is having the
worst vocation . . . a lonely frustrating work which is never as
good as you want it to be."

The Sound and the Fury had first been the sudden opening
up of a boundless field of possibilities, the happy vertigo of a
creation still innocent and unaware of its limitations, whose
movement bore Faulkner along in quick elation, as if he were
the entranced beholder of his own inventions. But once the
wonder of this privileged first moment was dispelled, and
the book was no longer the bright mirage of desire but a
work in progress, doubt and anxiety took over. And when

Faulkner looked back on what he had accomplished, he knew that his work was "still not finished," that the story he so wanted to tell, the only one to his eyes that was really worth the telling, was still to be told.

The Sound and the Fury was Faulkner's first great creative adventure. It assured him at once a major place in what has been, since Hawthorne, Poe, and Melville, the great tradition of failure in American literature. Like them and like other modern writers, from Flaubert and Mallarmé through Joyce, Kafka, Musil, and Beckett, it led him to the experience of the impossible. According to Faulkner himself, failure was the common fate of all writers of his generation: "All of us failed to match our dream of perfection." Whether the blame falls on the artist or on his medium, language, everything happens as though the writing process could never be completed, as though it could only be the gauging of a lack. Creation then ceases to be a triumphant gesture of assertion; it resigns itself to be the record of its errors, trials and defeats, the chronicle of its successive miscarriages, the inscription of the very impossibility from which it springs.

Hence an increased self-reflexiveness. Novels tend to turn into extended metaphors for the hazardous game of their writing. Novelists no longer seek to give a semblance of order to the chaos of life by relying on well-rounded characters and well-made plots. Instead of following a logical sequential pattern, events are subordinated to the process of the fictitious discourse itself as it takes shape, or fails to do so—unfolding, infolding, progressing, regressing, turning in on itself, spiraling, endlessly doubling back on itself in a never-completed quest for form and meaning. What is told then is not a story in the traditional sense, but the venture of its telling: the novel becomes the narrative of an impossible narrative. Commenting upon *The Man Without Qualities*, Robert Musil observed that "what the story of this novel amounts to is that the story which it should tell is not told." Faulkner might have said as much of *The Sound and the Fury*. The fragments of his story do not cohere into a unified scheme; they flout our expectations of order and significance. We have to accept them as such, in all their random brokenness and intriguing opaqueness, or rather we must join the author in his effort "to draw his disparate materials together, to compel his fiction into discovery of the unity of its seemingly opposed parts." For *The Sound and the Fury* is as much the locus as the product of its gestation.

—André Bleikasten, *The Most Splendid Failure: Faulkner's* The Sound and the Fury (Bloomington, IL: Indiana University Press, 1976), pp. 49–51

❖

LYNN GARTRELL LEVINS ON *THE SOUND AND THE FURY* AS CHIVALRIC ROMANCE

[Lynn Gartrell Levins is an author and literary critic whose works include *Faulkner's Heroic Design* (1976), from which the following is extracted. Levins examines *The Sound and the Fury* as a chivalric romance and discusses Quentin's shortcomings as the hero of the novel.]

If Quentin is unable to fulfill the obligations of his chivalric code, still he is unwilling to renounce that code. When he recognizes the impasse between life as it is lived by the Compsons and his own principles of honor and gallantry, he takes his life. It is as Mr. Compson had predicted—that Quentin will not commit suicide until he comes "to believe that even she [Caddy] was not quite worth despair." Although by all practical standards Quentin fails to live up to the heroic role, nevertheless Faulkner's fullest sympathy is with the quester; Quentin's chivalric attitude is to be positively evaluated against Dalton Ames's pronouncement on women which immediately follows his confrontation with Quentin: "They're all bitches." Faulkner's attitude toward his young protagonist is further clarified by his presentation of another Compson who patterns her conduct after the code of chivalry. The role to which Caroline Compson adapts her behavior—with more than a little joy, one must think—is the stereotyped role of the southern lady who is placed on a pedestal. The fact that she is one of those "delicately nurtured Southern ladies" allows Mrs. Compson the excuse to indulge herself in her numerous attacks of hypochondria. As with Quentin the role commands certain behavior, and so Benjy, who was named at birth after her own family, must be rechristened upon her discovery that he is an idiot so as not to bring shame to the Bascomb line. Similarly, when Mrs. Compson sees the youth kissing her fifteen-year-old Caddy, she reacts as she believes her image demands: "And all the next day she went around the house in a black dress and veil . . . crying and saying her little daughter was dead." If Mrs. Compson presents a humorous picture garbed in her mourning dress, confident that God will not flout her because she is, after all, a lady, she has none of the author's sympathy that is sometimes associated with a comic presentation. The significant difference between Quentin and his mother in terms of their chivalric pattern of behavior is that Quentin retains the conception of the morally valid principles which underlies this code of conduct while Mrs. Compson does not. She willingly accepts the devoted service and protection due a southern lady, since nothing could be more pleasing to her lazy, self-centered nature; at the same time she relegates to Dilsey the matriarch's role of family stabilizer and moral center. The result of Mrs. Compson's withholding from her family the love and affection, the attention and the discipline they need is revealed in Quentin's poignant cry before he drowns himself in the Charles River: *"If I'd just had a mother so I could say Mother Mother."*

—Lynn Gartrell Levins, *Faulkner's Heroic Design* (Athens, GA: University of Georgia Press, 1976), pp. 132–133

❧

GARY LEE STONUM ON THE ORIGINS OF *THE SOUND AND THE FURY*

[Gary Lee Stonum (b. 1947) is an associate professor of English at Case Western Reserve University and the editor of *Pieces: A Journal of Short Fiction*. In the following extract, taken from *Faulkner's Career: An Internal Literary History* (1979), Stonum examines the origins of *The Sound and the Fury* in earlier works by Faulkner and compares his efforts to present an image, rather than a narrative, of the Compson family.]

For all the advances it represents over the early fiction, *The Sound and the Fury* adheres to many of the goals and assumptions articulated in *Mosquitoes*, and there is reason to believe that the book began as an attempt to practice them unequivocally. Faulkner's numerous comments about the composition of *The Sound and the Fury* consistently emphasize the things in it that most resemble his earlier, image-based art. (To many of his readers and critics, Faulkner's convictions about the intentions and achievements of the novel have seemed curiously at odds with the actual text, but for the moment we are interested only in how the book can be seen to resemble his earlier work.) In virtually every statement Faulkner made in thirty years of speaking about the gestation of the novel, he insisted that it began with the luminous image of Caddy Compson and with the situation on the day of Damuddy's death. As Caddy was envisioned in the pastoral landscape at the branch and later peering in at the funeral, she became for Faulkner an image of the ideal beauty so often envisioned in the poetry. "To me she was the beautiful one, she was my heart's darling. That's what I wrote the book about . . . to try to tell, try to draw the picture of Caddy."

Notice that Faulkner abandons a narrative term, "tell," for a pictorial one. The goal remains the drawing of the static image. To the extent that his aim in *The Sound and the Fury* is primarily "to make myself a beautiful and tragic little girl," the book operates under the older method. It seeks an ideal beauty through a single fixed and splendid image, Caddy Compson as a little girl on a particular day. As in the poetry, this ideal is to be seen only indirectly. We see her only through the eyes of her brothers. More important, we discover her significance not directly through the effects on them of her presence but indirectly and negatively through the suffering and intense longing occasioned by her absence.

Moreover, the conception of the scenes on the day of Damuddy's death suggests the pictorial method of *Soldiers' Pay*. At the branch and later outside the Compson house, the children are arranged in a tableau of postures and spatial relationships with Caddy at the center. Very little occurs in the novel to modify the tableau; we get the essential, unchanging meaning of each character in a scene occurring twenty years before most of the others in the novel. Jason's moral isolation and his self-defeating selfishness are visible in his posture, hands jammed in his pockets, and later when he trips over his own feet. Quentin's futile desire to protect and to dominate his sister appears in his reaction to her wetting her dress and in his constant lagging behind in resistance to her leadership. Benjy's dependence on Caddy is evident when she squats in the water before him to soothe and hush his fears. Lastly, Caddy's tenderness is represented by the affectionate attention to Benjy, and her boldness by the insistence on climbing the tree to view the funeral.

The tableau is partly duplicated on a completely different level by the structural relationships of the novel's first three sections. Carried to completion, the duplication would contribute to a singularly static and self-enclosed method. Even as we moved through the three sections, we would proceed as though from one vantage point to another on a grouped configuration of statues, only to find that our vantage points, so Faulkner insists, the intent is to give us an increasingly clearer view of Caddy and the ideal she represents.

—Gary Lee Stonum, *Faulkner's Career* (Ithaca, NY: Cornell University Press, 1979), pp. 75–77

❖

WARWICK WADLINGTON ON *THE SOUND AND THE FURY* AS TRAGEDY

[Warwick Wadlington (b. 1938) is a professor of English at the University of Texas at Austin. He is the author of *The Confidence Game in American Literature* (1975). In the following extract, Wadlington looks at *The Sound and the Fury* in the tradition of classical and modern literary tragedy.]

In the same year that Joseph Wood Krutch made his famous claim that tragedy was contrary to the modern temper, William Faulkner published a paradoxical refutation. Krutch sought to define and decry his age by appealing to a traditional standard. *The Sound and the Fury* shows that the standard of tragedy contains the logic of its own failure. Yet critics have typically discussed the novel as if it could be described by some comparatively stable model, apart from the debate over the possibility of tragedy.

In the post-Enlightenment, pathos has become the term of contradistinction to tragedy. According to the most widespread view, tragedy involves suffering that results mainly from the protagonist's action, which is usually persistent, decisive—heroic. The mode of pathos, by contrast, is said to involve a relatively passive suffering, not springing from action but inflicted by circumstances. In terms of the linked root meanings of pathos (passion, suffering), tragedy is held to be pathos resulting from heroic action.

The stress on action, legitimized by Aristotle's poetics and ethics, was part of the general cultural defense of responsible human endeavor from the philosophy of mechanistic determinism. For many, the horror of a universe of mere physical motion could be summed up as an oppressive passivity in which, as Matthew Arnold wrote, "there is everything to be endured, nothing to be done." The emphasis on the difference between tragedy and pathos—that is, between action and passivity—was thus fundamentally polemic in nature if not always in tone. By the beginning of Faulkner's career, tragedy had become *the* prestigious literary genre. Pathos had largely lost its neutral, descriptive connotation and was increasingly a term of denigration, especially in the form "pathetic." Influential theorists like the New Humanists upheld a conservative position by accentuating this difference. "Tragic" had become a weapon useful for excoriating the naturalists, the "Freudians," and "the school of cruelty." Yet important writers since at least Dostoevski had reflected the modern idea of passive man while also seeking to reformulate the possibilities of human action. Sometimes these possibilities were found at the very center of apparent passivity, where pathos is describable by its etymological kin, pathology.

But action is not the only usual discriminator of tragedy. In Aristotle's account, the mimesis of action arouses in the audience certain passions and subjects them to catharsis. A catastrophe is instrumental in effecting this tragic relief. In pathos, by contrast, there is no final crisis, no resolution and emotional disburdening. Passion is the inconclusive fate.

The traditional conception (or kind) of tragedy we consider here focuses typically on the drastic either/or to which life may be reduced, in a tightening spiral of narrowing options. *Antigone, Hamlet, Moby-Dick,* and *The Mayor of Casterbridge*, for example, follow this pattern, as does the *Oresteia* until the last-moment reversal. Hegel's theory speaks powerfully to such cases by treating tragedy as the collision of contradictory views. In Hegel's Absolute, variances are merely *differences*, but when concertized in human action they become contradictory *oppositions* liable to tragic conflict.

Hegel aside for the moment, the idea of contradictory opposition itself points to connections between pairs of concepts that seem simply opposed—the modern temper and the heroic, and tragedy and pathos. In *The Heroic Temper,* Bernard Knox authoritatively defines the hallmark of Sophocles' tragic heroes: "their watchword is: 'he who is not with me is against me.'" Sophoclean tragedy dramatizes the usually unavailing attempts of advisors to persuade the intransigent heroes—Ajax, Antigone, Electra, Oedipus, Philoctetes—to abandon the self-destructive polarization of their outraged self-esteem against the world. The Sophoclean heroic outlook is the relatively rare consequence of a severe threat to personal worth that arouses the exceptional person to this uncompromisingly dichotomous attitude. Let us imagine a case, however, in which the essential binary quality of this temper became widespread. Such would be the result if dichotomy were the usual structure of consciousness. The protagonist then would be surrounded by those who, at bottom, experience life in no less starkly divisive terms than he or she does on the tragic occasion. Rather than being a monitory, awe-inspiring anomaly as in Sophocles, polarization would be a constant daily potential. The result would be strikingly different from Sophoclean tragedy, though bearing the prototype's mark. The ironic product is the odd suspension of heroic temper and "unheroism" in tone and mood of *The Sound and the Fury.*

—Warwick Wadlington, "*The Sound and the Fury*: A Logic of Tragedy," *American Literature* 53, No. 3 (November 1981): 409–411

❖

THADIUS M. DAVIS ON THE COMPSONS' RACISM AND SOUTHERN IDENTITY

[Thadius M. Davis (b. 1944) is the author of numerous works on African-American literature, including *Nella Larsen, Novelist of the Harlem Renaissance: A Woman's Life Unveiled* (1994). Davis has also edited a number of volumes on black writers. In the following extract, taken from *Faulkner's "Negro": Art and the Southern Context* (1983), Davis explores the significance of the Compsons' perceptions about self and other in light of their racist views of blacks.]

At the center of Jason's portrait, and his dilemma, is a complex problem regarding perception of self and others that is intrinsic to Faulkner's art: the intellectual and emotional duality of southerners which is most forcefully revealed in the double standards of race. Having its historical origins in slavery, in postbellum society this duality pertains directly to the spread of

"Jim Crow" which insured that the two already existing societies, one white and the other black, would be opposed to each other. Faulkner's fiction relies upon differences between values, attitudes, beliefs, or hopes of white and black life. His characters who most avidly uphold racial distinctions cannot acknowledge a common humanity. Jason, for example, voices one of the commonplace assumptions resulting from this view: "When people act like niggers, no matter who they are the only thing to do is to treat them like a nigger." Jason uses "people" as a synonym for whites. A "nigger," according to Jason's logic, is not a person and so cannot behave like "people."

Because of this fragmented condition, Faulkner's white and black characters develop the ability to live mutually exclusive lives, which acknowledge the existence but not the validity of the other. As a result, they are suspended in moral and intellectual contradictions. They learn to live with a false sense of harmony by partially blinding themselves to reality. Although their separate worlds sometimes show signs of consolidation beyond superficial contact, such signs prove misleading. Faulkner's whites especially are rivetted to rituals and manners; their relationships remain fixed and static. Change is frustrated by impotency and fear—outgrowths of an isolation dictated by historical division. In *The Sound and the Fury*, Faulkner presents the Gibsons seemingly within reach of the Compsons, who need new models for saving themselves; however, he maintains implicitly that the Gibsons are inaccessible to the whites. He suggests that the Compsons cannot learn from the example of the Negro because they do not see the example. The partitioning of their society distorts their vision of life and themselves.

The girl Quentin in her relationship with Dilsey is Faulkner's most dramatic rendering of duality in a divided world. Her contradictory feelings toward the black servant prevent her from receiving the maternal comfort she seeks. In Benjy's section, Dilsey defends Quentin against Jason's insinuations: "*Hush your mouth, Jason, Dilsey said. She went and put her arm around Quentin. Sit down, honey, Dilsey said. He ought to be shamed of himself, throwing what aint your fault up to you.*" But Quentin responds by pushing Dilsey away. And in Jason's monologue,

Quentin, stung by Jason's taunt ("You damn little slut"), calls out to Dilsey for comfort: "'Dilsey,' she says, 'Dilsey I want my mother.' Dilsey went to her. 'Now, now,' she says, 'He aint gwine so much as lay his hand on you while Ise here.'" Yet when Dilsey touches Quentin, she is immediately rebuffed. Quentin knocks her hand down and cries out, "'You damn old nigger.'"

Simultaneously, the white girl reaches out for Dilsey as a mother substitute and rejects "the nigger" who could never be her mother.

⟨. . .⟩ Even more than the other Compsons, Quentin, narrator of "June Second 1910," exemplifies the stultifying results of a fractured world, because in the process of learning to live in that world, he suffers an irreparable fragmentation of self. Quentin is an exaggeration of the southern gentleman, whose mind, no longer creative, is locked into sterile types and kinds, codes and manners. His unfailing attention to details of stylized behavior and customs, even when they lack meaning in social interaction, illustrates the extent of his division. His slavery to social conduct blocks off reality, particularly at the end of his monologue when he brushes his teeth and looks for a freshman hat before going to drown himself. His actions point to an evasion of reality by sacrificing clear perception and honest thinking.

Quentin's thoughts about blacks, however, most clearly reveal that his personality, his pattern of thought and behavior are rigidly shaped by an escape mechanism involving the fragmentation of self. Throughout his monologue Quentin returns time and time again to "niggers": Deacon, bootblacks, nigger sayings, anonymous niggers, Louis Hatcher, the Gibsons. Even in the simple matter of getting on northern street cars, he notices immediately whether or not "niggers" are aboard. Despite his dwelling on blacks and his seeming awareness of them, Quentin still observes, "I used to think that a Southerner had to be always conscious of niggers." He believes that he is not, and the irony lies in the discrepancy between what he believes about himself, and his world, and what his thoughts and actions reveal. Quentin's preoccupation with blacks represents his unacknowledged awareness of the other, alternative possibility for life in a divided world—the world which Quentin

as southerner transposes to Massachusetts. The Negro popu-
lating Quentin's monologue becomes a strategic figure for what
is missing in Quentin's white world and a subtle projection of
his own internal state.

—Thadius M. Davis, *Faulkner's "Negro": Art and the Southern
Context* (Baton Rouge, LA: Louisiana State University Press,
1983), pp. 92–94

❖

GAIL L. MORTIMER ON THE RHETORIC OF QUENTIN'S MONOLOGUE

[Gail L. Mortimer (b. 1943) is an author, literary critic,
and Faulkner scholar. Her publications include
*Faulkner's Rhetoric of Loss: A Study in Perception and
Meaning* (1983), from which the following extract was
taken. Mortimer examines Faulkner's language and
style in the Quentin section of *The Sound and the Fury*
as the character's attempt to control time.]

The rhetoric of Quentin Compson's monologue in *The Sound
and the Fury* ⟨. . .⟩ reveals the modes of perception of one
explicitly preoccupied with the passage of time. Again, we have
before us a slightly exaggerated instance of language reflecting
a constant awareness of change and loss—by virtue of the
obsessions that dominate everything Quentin does—but we
see a perceptual style that, nevertheless, illuminates our understanding of more typical ways of looking at the world characteristic of even the omniscient narrators in Faulkner's stories.
As Quentin experiences his world flowing out of control, his
perceptions increasingly involve the spatializing of all of his
sensations and thoughts in a manifest attempt to manage
reality through the illusion of control that is innate to vision.
Quentin, through Faulkner, virtually geometrizes the objects he
encounters to control their relationships to one another and
himself, and his story abounds with horizontal and vertical
lines, oblique lines, bridges and lanes, frames (mirrors, door-

ways, watch faces), enclosed spaces or spaces that feel like vacuums, and rhythmically regular segments of both time and space. The world itself undermines his efforts to keep things stable as it fragments, flows, and changes through time despite Quentin's vigilance. From the first words onward, Quentin's monologue expresses his struggle with time as he searches for timeless (that is, purely spatial, stable) modes of perception. Time is transformed into a place to be—"then I was in time again, hearing the watch"—but it is also his enemy because it is where change irrevocably occurs.

Quentin's radical spatializing is an attempt to reverse the effects of time, specifically to undo the changes that have occurred in Caddy as her emerging sexuality has left him behind by totally changing their relationship. Quentin wants to recapture their reliance on one another and their intimacy by controlling and turning back time. As we shall see, he accomplishes this symbolically in his death.

Among the perceptions that dominate the monologue are those of Quentin's nihilistic father, Jason, which Quentin struggles unsuccessfully to deny. In Jason Compson's view, man is a pathetic combination of molecules and experiences doomed to fade quickly into anonymity and meaninglessness. Quentin tries to establish "importance" in his universe—a semblance of immortality, something that does not fade with time—but he is undermined by his father's vision of things: "Father was teaching us that all men are just accumulations dolls stuffed with sawdust swept up from the trash heaps where all previous dolls had been thrown away the sawdust flowing from what wound in what side that not for me died not;" "Man the sum of his climatic [sic] experiences Father said. Man the sum of what have you. A problem in impure properties carried tediously to an unvarying nil: stalemate of dust and desire." Instead of flesh and blood, inanimate entities coalesce to form mankind. There is no hope of achieving identity or importance in such a world, and we recognize in Quentin's efforts to reify such notions as honor, virginity, and his imagined incest with Caddy—all of which, because they are insubstantial, cannot fade—attempts to defy the dissolution that besets everything around him. Jason recognizes the illusoriness of such an imaginative control of one's perceptions: "you wanted to sublimate a piece of natural human folly into a horror and then exorcise it;" "you are not thinking of finitude you are contemplating an apotheosis in which a temporary state of mind will become symmetrical above the flesh and aware both of itself and of the flesh it will not quite discard . . . you cannot bear to think that someday it will no longer hurt you like this."

This dissolution of Quentin's world is also suggested in the precariousness of his sense of self, especially evident in his relationship with his own shadow, that penumbral part of himself that he seems to regard as perversely having an existence of its own. A walk becomes an occasion to trick his shadow into merging with water or other shadows, to trample it into the pavement and the dust, and to walk on its belly. As a dimension of his own surface, Quentin's shadow is important because it shows us his preoccupation with control, literally with self-control. Perhaps his shadow, with its darkness and fluidity, represents the dark, soft, feminine aspect of Quentin and, as such, threatens him with a loss of his sense of himself; this meaning would certainly be consistent with our understanding of the similar dilemma in Joe Christmas. The shadow's easy merging with ground, water, trees, and other shadows through its softness and malleability suggests its affinities with the feminine. Quentin is only able to react to its flowing by asserting rigidity and control, by successfully "tricking" it. It is clear, though, that his shadow, as part of his surface, evades definition and management. It preserves its essential fluidity, and, in doing so, serves as an appropriate focus for Quentin's absorption with the existence and potential annihilation of his own identity. His death plunges him into fusion with his shadow: "Niggers say a drowned man's shadow was watching for him in the water all the time."

—Gail L. Mortimer, *Faulkner's Rhetoric of Loss: A Study in Perceptions and Meaning* (Austin, TX: University of Texas Press, 1983), pp. 62–64

❖

JESSIE MCGUIRE COFFEE ON BENJAMIN AS A CHRIST FIGURE

[Jessie McGuire Coffee is an author and literary critic. In the following extract, taken from *Faulkner's Un-Christianlike Christians* (1983), Coffee discusses Benjamin as an involuntary and unqualified Christ figure.]

Benjamin is the sacrificial figure in the Compson household, considered from the viewpoint of Biblical allusions and symbolism. Although an idiot, Benjy is a sympathetic character. First, the thirty-three-year-old man is presented as a child. Ben's narrative (actually unspoken, since he cannot talk) has the simplicity of the rambling discourse of a small child, as when he says, "the dark came back." Ben is described as having blond bangs and a "sweet blue gaze." He plays in his make-believe graveyard like a child. And others, especially Dilsey, treat him as a babe:

> Dilsey led Ben to the bed and drew him down beside her and she held him, rocking back and forth, wiping his drooling mouth upon the hem of her skirt. "Hush. Dilsey got you."

Again, at mealtime, "Ben could manage solid food pretty well for himself, though even now, with cold food before him, Dilsey tied a cloth about his neck."

Second, Ben is more than a child: he is "de Lawd's chile." He is the innocent, natural boy who likes frogs, cows, smoke, the pasture; he dislikes perfume, especially on his sister Caddy, preferring that she smell "like trees." As an innocent, Benjy perceives the truth when others do not; for instance, he knows that Caddy's perfume is connected with her sexual escapades. At Caddy's wedding Benjy wails loudly. His brother Quentin later speaks of Benjy's reaction as being "out of the mouths of babes." The boy's response to the unfortunate union was the correct one. Caddy's marriage was doomed to fail.

Third, Benjy is a sacrifice for the faults of others. He obviously has some of the chronology of Christ, and he is linked metaphorically with Benjamin (son of Jacob), who was held hostage in Egypt. (In Faulkner the expression becomes "sold into Egypt.") Ben's brother Quentin feels that the idiot has been abused in some way: he calls Benjamin "child of my sorrowful," which suggests Isaiah's "a man of sorrows and acquainted with grief," who was "led as a lamb to the slaughter" but opened not his mouth. Benjy is a sacrificial figure in that he loses his masculinity, he loses his beloved sister, and he, who is terrified by any change in routine, loses his familiar surroundings when he sent to the asylum.

But Benjamin is not a satisfactory Christ-figure, nor is he meant to be. His mental state does not qualify him for such a role. His sacrifice is an involuntary one, whereas Christ chose his propitiatory office. In the pastoral tradition, however, Benjamin is a sympathetic character in that, first, he is the innocent child who sees truth more clearly than do his elders; second, he is the fool who sees truly, or, as one of the Negroes says, "He know a lot more than folks thinks." And third, he is the scapegoat who suffers for the sins of others. But like Dilsey, Benjamin cannot attain salvation for those around him. He can only suffer.

—Jessie McGuire Coffee, *Faulkner's Un-Christianlike Christians* (Ann Arbor, MI: UMI Research Press, 1983), pp. 38–39

❖

JAMES M. COX ON LITERARY FORM AND LOSS IN *THE SOUND AND THE FURY*

[James M. Cox (b. 1925), the Avalon Professor at Dartmouth College, is a coauthor of *The Third Day at Gettysburg: Pickett's Charge* (1959) and the author of *Mark Twain: The Fate of Humor* (1966). In the following extract, Cox explores the structure and form of *The Sound and the Fury* as enabling the reader to experience loss.]

To encounter The Sound and the Fury is, first of all, to be lost. That loss is, for me, fully equal in importance to all the loss that the book is about. You will remember that, in what we have inaccurately but inevitably call the Benjy section, Benjy and Luster are by the golf course looking for a quarter—or rather Luster is looking for it. We are ultimately to learn that the golf course itself is part of the land the Compsons have lost; and we learn that Benjy has lost his sister, that Luster is about to lose his chance to go to the show, that the golfers have lost their balls. And we are to learn that Caddy has lost her virginity, that Quentin has lost his life, that Jason has lost his money, that the Compsons have been in a long descent of loss in a world that has lost its war and that still suffers one long continuity of loss. All those losses are what we are going to discover—but we discover them only because we have first been lost ourselves. If Faulkner hadn't, by means of his great form, made us experience being lost, we would only have been reading about loss instead of discovering it.

We are, of course, in that first section, lost in *time*, even though the sections are temporally denominated, as if Faulkner were determined to set the time only to emphasize how lost in time we were to be. We are lost because the idiot narrator, in relation to us, seems free in time, shifting abruptly from one spot of time to another. Actually, Benjy is ruthlessly held, not in time but in an iron principle of association that constantly transcends progressional time. What the book makes us do from the outset is to begin a long process of reconstruction of the so-called rational sequence of "real" time that has so rudely been taken away. There are of course abundant associations present in Benjy's account that enable us to reconstruct our rational version of time—a version possessing all the iron principles as well as the irony that Benjy's helpless submission to association has. Obsessed by Caddy and the loss of Caddy, Benjy is helpless but no more helpless than we are to our own obsession with "logical" sequence.

⟨. . .⟩ Lost in Benjy's consciousness, we hear the voices of his world, and, if we are not too obsessed with regaining our lost temporal sequence, we feel the poetry of that world. When we enter Quentin's section, though associational obsession continues to fracture sequence, we gain an even richer dimension of feeling. What was bewilderment in the Benjy section beautifully and steadily grows into a sense of sympathy. Quentin is as obsessed as Benjy, but his obsession is different. Knowing what time is, he is nonetheless helpless before the intrusions of his past, and we now feel them as we could not—because we did not know how to—in the first section. Possessing both will and deliberation, Quentin can plan his suicide—though few readers on a first reading would know exactly what he is planning. Because time and will and choice occupy the foreground of Quentin's interior consciousness, all the loss in Quentin's past is perpetually at the threshold of inrushing upon his mind. Whereas all time is present to Benjy, Quentin holds on to present time, allocating it through the day as well as marking its advancing shadow on the dial of his life as he determines to stop it forever in order to ward off all the past and all the loss that preys upon him as powerfully as it preys on Benjy. For Quentin's father, *was* is the saddest of all words, but for Quentin it is *again*. Anguished in relation to what he knows is past and helpless to prevent its intrusions, Quentin can see only one repetition—but the point is that he can see it, and see in it the hopelessness that it will bring.

With Jason we seem to come out of the pain and poetry and loss—our own, as readers, as well as that of the characters. To be sure, we are still in the consciousness of a character, but it is, consciousness in the form of voice rather than of mind. Because Jason's vernacular objectifies his character, we hear his own voice in a way we never heard Benjy's or Quentin's. Moreover, we are brought toward the realm of the common sense that had been withheld in the first two sections of the book. Returning us to the familiar categories of temporal sequence, Jason's consciousness represents a decisive clearing of the confusion.

—James M. Cox, "Humor as Vision in Faulkner," *Faulkner and Humor,* eds. Doreen Fowler and Ann J. Abadie (Jackson, MS: University Press of Mississippi, 1986), pp. 5–7

❖

Deborah Clarke on Caddy Compson as Sister and Mother

[Deborah Clarke (b. 1956) is an author and literary critic with a special interest in feminist issues. Her publications include *Robbing the Mother: Women in Faulkner* (1994), from which the following extract is taken. Clarke argues that *The Sound and the Fury* is less about Caddy Compson than about her brothers' responses to her complex sexuality as both sister and mother.]

This is not a novel about Caddy, despite Faulkner's claims, but about her brothers' responses to her, about how men deal with women and sexuality. In fact, Faulkner's almost obsessive insistence on Caddy's importance begins to sound defensive, an apology, perhaps, for essentially writing her out of the text. Caddy's linguistic absence from the novel undercuts her centrality in a text formed and sustained by voice. If she is his heart's darling, why does she not rate a section of the novel, the chance to tell her own story? But Faulkner goes further than just silencing Caddy; he ties her silence to her beauty, her femininity, and claims that "Caddy was still to me too beautiful and too moving to reduce her to telling what was going on, that it would be more passionate to see her through somebody else's eyes." David Minter has suggested that Faulkner found "indirection" a useful strategy "for approaching forbidden scenes, uttering forbidden words, committing dangerous acts." Yet the "forbidden words" and "dangerous acts" appear not to be Caddy's but those of her brothers: Quentin's incestuous desires, Jason's criminality, and Benjy's groping for the language "to say" which culminates in attempted rape. Indirection may approach male forbidden desires, but it does not approach Caddy except as the direct object of those desires.

Particularly in Faulkner's work, however, silence does not necessarily confer marginality. Paul Lilly has called Caddy's silence "a hallmark of the perfect language that Faulkner the artist knows can never be realized but which he knows he must 'keep on working, trying again' to reach." But why must it be women who speak the perfect silence instead of language, even imperfect language? Linda Wagner argues that, despite their full or partial silences, Caddy and her mother control the narrative:

> Linguistic theory would define the narrator of any fiction as the person whose speech act dominates the telling, yet Caddy and Caroline Compson are in many ways essential narrators of the Compson story. So much of their language, so much of their verbal presence, emanates through the novel that they are clearly and vividly drawn. Rather than being given one section, they take the novel entire.

They are indeed "clearly and vividly drawn." Yet the fact remains that they are drawn rather than draw-ers, constructed rather than constructor, while the Compson brothers draw not only themselves but also "their" women.

Caddy's voice may never be restored, but the evidence of her physical substance remains. If her "speech act" does not dominate the text, her creative act does. Caddy's presence makes itself known less through her voice than through her body and its literal replication. Her physical procreation essentially engenders the linguistic acts which form the novel, thereby making this text, in a sense, her child. Yet it is difficult to claim that she "mothers" the novel when the process of mothering—and, particularly, Caddy's participation in that process—is hardly presented within the book as a triumphant creative experience. Her abandonment of her daughter to Jason and his malicious exploitation seriously undermines both her idealized status and her maternal position. While she serves as an admirable if temporary mother to Benjy, her treatment of Miss Quentin merits her no consideration as Mother of the Year. Faulkner has robbed the mother not just of her voice but her maternity. Because the brothers control the terms of the narrative, Caddy exists as sister rather than mother.

The problem, however, is that she serves as a mother as well, not just to Benjy but to all of her brothers, who find themselves confronted with problematic maternal ties to both their biological and symbolic mothers. Thus while their narratives, except for Jason's, lack the overt condemnation of Caddy which they all display towards Caroline (and even Jason saves his strongest complaints for Miss Quentin, displacing much of his resentment toward Caddy onto her daughter), they also reveal their unbreakable ties to Caddy, ties which deny them full control over their own identities. By his indirection, Faulkner has allowed Caddy to approach the position of all-powerful and all-encroaching mother rather than simply mother of Miss Quentin. Doubly abandoned, first by Caroline and then by Caddy, the Compson men achieve a kind of revenge in fixing both, in allowing each woman to be defined only through the perspective of her son/brother.

They fail to score a significant victory, however, because just as each brother inscribes his vision of Caddy, he also finds himself defined through his own relation to her. Quentin is trapped by being the weaker older brother to a powerful sister, by his own attraction to her, and by his sexual innocence as opposed to her experience:

> youve never done that have you
> what done what
> that what I have what I did

Jason struggles against his sense of being unimportant and unloved, the brother whom Caddy never valued. Benjy cannot perceive himself as anything other than connected to Caddy, as his entire life constitutes an elegy of her loss. As both a presence and absence, Caddy's maternity determines the fate of the Compson family.

—Deborah Clarke, *Robbing the Mother: Women in Faulkner* (Jackson, MS: University Press of Mississippi, 1994), pp. 20–22

❖

Works by William Faulkner

The Marble Faun. 1924.

Soldiers' Pay. 1926.

Sherwood Anderson and Other Famous Creoles (editor). 1926.

Mosquitoes. 1927.

Sartoris. 1929.

The Sound and the Fury. 1929.

As I Lay Dying. 1930.

Sanctuary. 1931.

These 13. 1931.

Idyll in the Desert. 1931.

Light in August. 1932.

Salmagundi. 1932.

This Earth. 1932.

Miss Zilphia Gant. 1932.

A Green Bough. 1933.

Doctor Martino and Other Stories. 1934.

Pylon. 1935.

Absalom, Absalom! 1936.

The Unvanquished. 1938.

The Wild Palms. 1939.

The Hamlet. 1940.

Go Down, Moses and Other Stories. 1942.

A Rose for Emily and Other Stories. 1945.

The Portable Faulkner. Ed. Malcolm Cowley. 1946.

Intruder in the Dust. 1948.

Knight's Gambit. 1949.

Collected Stories. 1950.

Notes on a Horsethief. 1951.

*Speech of Acceptance Upon the Award of the Nobel
   Prize for Literature.* 1951.

Requiem for a Nun. 1951.

Mirrors of Chartre Street. 1953.

The Faulkner Reader. 1954

A Fable. 1954.

Big Woods. 1955.

Jealousy and Episode: Two Stories. 1955.

New Orleans Sketches. Ed. Ichiro Nishizaki. 1955.

The Segregation Decisions (with Benjamin E. Mays and
   Cecil Sims). 1956.

Faulkner at Nagano. Ed. Robert A. Jelliffe. 1956.

The Town. 1957.

Three Famous Novels. 1958.

The Mansion. 1959.

The Reivers. 1962.

Selected Short Stories. 1962.

Early Prose and Poetry. Ed. Carvel Collins. 1962.

The Faulkner-Cowley File: Letters and Memories 1944–1962
   (with Malcolm Cowley). 1966.

Essays, Speeches and Public Letters. Ed. James B. Meriwether. 1966.

The Wishing Tree. 1967.

Flags in the Dust. Ed. Douglas Day. 1973.

Selected Letters. Ed. Joseph Blotner. 1977.

Mayday. 1977.

Helen: A Courtship and Mississippi Poems. 1981.

Faulkner's MGM Screenplays. Ed. Bruce F. Kawin. 1982.

Elmer. Ed. Dianne L. Cox. 1984.

Country Lawyer and Other Stories for the Screen. 1987.

Stallion Road: A Screenplay (with Louis D. Brodsky and Robert W. Hamblin). 1989.

Works About William Faulkner and *The Sound and the Fury*

Adams, Richard P. *Faulkner: Myth and Motion*. Princeton, NJ: Princeton University Press, 1968.

Anderson, Charles. "Faulkner's Moral Center." *Etudes anglaises* 7, no. 1 (January 1954): 48–58.

Aswell, Duncan. "The Recollections and the Blood: Jason's Role in *The Sound and the Fury*." *Mississippi Quarterly* 21, no. 3 (Summer 1968): 211–18.

Backman, Melvin. *Faulkner, The Major Years: A Critical Study*. Bloomington, IN: Indiana University Press, 1966.

Bassett, John E., ed. *William Faulkner: The Critical Heritage*. London: Routledge & Kegan Paul, 1975.

Baum, Katherine B. "'The Beautiful One': Caddy Compson as Heroine of *The Sound and the Fury*." *Modern Fiction Studies* 13, no. 1 (Spring 1967): 33–44.

Bowling, Lawrence. "Faulkner: Technique in *The Sound and the Fury*." *Kenyon Review* 10, no. 4 (Autumn 1948): 555–66.

_____. "Faulkner and the Theme of Innocence." *Kenyon Review* 20, no. 3 (Summer 1958): 466–87.

Brooks, Cleanth. "Primitivism in *The Sound and the Fury*." In *English Institute Essays*, ed. Alan S. Downer. New York: Columbia University Press, 1954, pp. 5–28.

Brown, Mary Cameron. "The Language of Chaos: Quentin Compson in *The Sound and the Fury*." *American Literature* 51, no. 4 (January 1954): 544–53.

Bryowski, Walter. *Faulkner's Olympian Laugh: Myth in the Novels.* Detroit: Wayne State University Press, 1968.

Cecil, L. Moffitt. "A Rhetoric for Benjy." *Southern Literary Journal* 3, no. 1 (Fall 1970): 32–46.

Cointreau, Maurice Edgar. *The Time of William Faulkner: A French View of Modern American Fiction.* Ed. and trans. George McMillan Reeves. Columbia: University of South Carolina Press, 1971.

Collins, Carvel. "The Interior Monologues of *The Sound and the Fury.*" In *English Institute Essays,* ed. Alan S. Downer. New York: Columbia University Press, 1954, pp 29–56.

Conder, John J. *Naturalism in American Fiction: The Classic Phase.* Lexington: University Press of Kentucky, 1984.

Cowan, Michael H., ed. *Twentieth-Century Interpretations of* The Sound and the Fury. Englewood Cliffs, NJ: Prentice-Hall, 1968.

Cowley, Malcolm. "Dilsey and the Compsons." *University of Mississippi Studies in English* 14 (1974): 79–97.

Dauner, Louise. "Quentin and the Walking Shadow: The Dilemma of Nature and Culture." *Arizona Quarterly* 21, no. 2 (Summer 1965): 159–71.

Foster, Ruel E. "Social Order and Disorder in Faulkner's Fiction." *Approach* 55 (Spring 1965): 20–28.

Geffen, Arthur. "Profane Time, Sacred Time, and Confederate Time in *The Sound and the Fury.*" *Studies in American Fiction* 2, no. 2 (Autumn 1974): 175–97.

Greer, Dorothy D. "Dilsey and Lucas: Faulkner's Use of the Negro as a Gauge of Moral Character." *The Emporia State Research Studies* 11, no. 1 (September 1962): 43–61.

Hunt, John W. *William Faulkner: Art in Theological Tension.* Syracuse, NY: Syracuse University Press, 1964.

Iser, Wolfgang. *The Implied Reader: Patterns of Communication from Bunyan to Beckett.* Baltimore: Johns Hopkins University Press, 1975.

Jehlen, Myra. *Class and Character in Faulkner's South.* New York: Columbia University Press, 1981.

Jenkins, Lee. *Faulkner and Black-White Relations: A Psychoanalytic Approach.* New York: Columbia University Press, 1981.

King, Richard H. *A Southern Renaissance: The Cultural Awakening of the American South, 1930–1955.* New York: Oxford University Press, 1980.

Kinney, Arthur F. *Faulkner's Narrative Poetics: Style as Vision.* Amherst, MA: University of Massachusetts Press, 1978.

La Londe, Christopher. *William Faulkner and the Rites of Passages.* Macon, GA: Mercer University Press, 1996.

Longley, John L. Jr. "'Who Never Had A Sister': A Reading of *The Sound and the Fury.*" *Mosaic* 7, no. 1 (Fall 1973): 35–53.

Messedi, Douglas. "The Problem of Time in *The Sound and the Fury:* A Critical Reassessment and Reinterpretation." *Southern Literary Journal* 6, no. 2 (Spring 1974): 19–41.

Minter, David. "Faulkner, Childhood, and the Making of *The Sound and the Fury.*" *American Literature* 51, no. 3 (November 1979): 376–93.

Peavy, Charles D. "Faulkner's Use of Folklore in *The Sound and the Fury.*" *Journal of American Folklore* 79, no. 313 (July–September 1966): 437–47.

Pikoulis, John. *The Art of William Faulkner.* London: Macmillan, 1982.

Polk, Noel. *An Editorial Handbook for William Faulkner's* The Sound and the Fury. New York: Garland, 1985.

Reed, Joseph W., Jr. *Faulkner's Narrative.* New Haven: Yale University Press, 1973.

Reesman, Jeanne Campbell. *American Designs: The Late Novels of James and Faulkner.* Philadelphia: University of Pennsylvania Press, 1991.

Ross, Stephen M. "The 'Loud World' of Quentin Compson." *Studies in the Novel* 7, no. 2 (Summer 1975): 245–57.

Slabey, Robert M. "The 'Romanticism' of *The Sound and the Fury.*" *Mississippi Quarterly* 16, no. 3 (Summer 1963): 146–59.

Slater, Judith. "Quentin's Tunnel Vision: Modes of Perception and Their Stylistic Realization in *The Sound and the Fury.*" *Literature and Psychology* 27, no. 1 (1977): 4–15.

Snead, James A. *Figures of Division: Faulkner's Major Novels.* New York: Methuen, 1986.

Traschen, Isodore. "The Tragic Form of *The Sound and the Fury.*" *Southern Review* 12, no. 4 (October 1976).

Wall, Carey. "*The Sound and the Fury*: The Emotional Center." *Midwest Quarterly* 11, no. 4 (Summer 1970): 371–87.

Warren, Robert Penn, ed. *Faulkner: A Collection of Critical Essays.* Englewood Cliffs, NJ: Prentice-Hall, 1966.

Weinstein, Phillip M. *The Cambridge Companion to William Faulkner.* Cambridge, MA: Cambridge University Press, 1995.

Index of
Themes and Ideas

21, 23, 24, 25, 26, 27–28, 29, 30, 31, 32, 33, 37, 39, 46, 47, 52, 66, 84–85, 89